HEATHERS IN COLOUR

Heathers

in Colour

Brian and Valerie Proudley

BLANDFORD PRESS · LONDON

First published in 1974
by Blandford Press Ltd
167 High Holborn, London WC1V 6PH

© Blandford Press 1974

ISBN 0 7137 0635 X

Printed in Great Britain by
Fletcher & Son Ltd, Norwich

CONTENTS

ACKNOWLEDGEMENTS

In taking the photographs we have travelled many miles both in Britain and Holland and in the course of so doing have met many kind people who have given every assistance and thus made the work even more pleasant. Our thanks to all of these.

Gardens photographed include the following, which are reproduced by courtesy of their owners: Azalealaan 34, Boskoop, Holland (Mr H. J. van de Laar); Bridgemere Nurseries Ltd, Woore, Cheshire (Mr John Ravenscroft); 'Champs Hill', Pulborough, Sussex (Mr and Mrs A. H. Bowerman); Harlow Car Gardens, Harrogate, Yorkshire (The Northern Horticultural Society); 'Meadows', Draycote, Rugby, Warwickshire (Mr and Mrs Raymond Law); Valley Garden, The Great Park, Windsor, Berkshire (The Crown Estate Commissioners); Von Gimborn Arboretum, Doorn, Holland (University of Utrecht); Wisley Garden, Ripley, Surrey (The Royal Horticultural Society).

Individual plants were also photographed in two of the leading heather specialists nurseries in Holland. These were: Fa. W. Haalboom & Zoon, Boomkwekerij 'Sempervirens', Driebergen-Rijsenburg and Fa. P. G. Zwijnenburg, Rijnveld 35, Boskoop.

Although most of the photographs are our own we have been greatly assisted by others who have kindly loaned transparencies from their own collections.

Our thanks are due to the following: Mr and Mrs A. H. Bowerman (Nos. 6, 75, 76, 99); Mr W. Haalboom (No. 8); The Heather Society (Nos. 94, 97).

Mr John F. Letts has also provided us with pictures of his former garden at Windlesham, Surrey (Nos. 15, 78, 90, 91, 100). The emphasis here was on heathers, and although when he took over the site it was a collection of neglected allotments, in the space of a few short years it became a show-place where visitors could wander and be able to view heathers planted as they should be. Several good plants had their origins here and many people went away inspired to grow heathers in a similar manner. Mr Letts has now moved to New Zealand where a garden on similar lines, but on a larger scale, is being developed.

FOREWORD

When, ten years ago, I was appointed Chairman of the newly-formed Heather Society, I felt it a duty to order heathers from as many growers as possible so that I could form an opinion of those best to deal with.

I sent an order to Aldenham Heathers, partly perhaps because my family had had a connection with Aldenham in Hertfordshire for many years. This firm was run by Brian and Valerie Proudley, and I soon formed a high opinion not only of the quality of their plants but of their keen and deep knowledge and appreciation of all forms of heathers.

The Proudleys have now moved to Gloucestershire and their business has expanded greatly. They are held in high regard by the committee of the Heather Society who have entrusted them with the arrangement of an annual display of heathers on behalf of the Society in the Royal Horticultural Society's hall.

A book on heathers and their cultivation by such authorities as the Proudleys must surely appeal to the growing number of gardeners who are planting heathers up and down the country, and abroad.

Sir John Charrington

METRIC CONVERSION TABLE

Distances (approx.)

0·3 m = 1 ft	2 m = 6 ft
0·5 m = 1½ ft	2·5 m = 8 ft
0·6 m = 2 ft	3 m = 10 ft
0·7 m = 2 ft	
0·8 m = 2½ ft	
1 m = 3 ft	1 m = 39·4 in.
1·5 m = 5 ft	1 m² = 10·8 sq ft

Sizes (approx.)

1 cm = ½ in.	15 cm = 6 in.
2 cm = ¾ in.	18 cm = 7 in.
3 cm = 1 in.	20 cm = 8 in.
4 cm = 1½ in.	23 cm = 9 in.
5 cm = 2 in.	25 cm = 10 in.
6 cm = 2¼ in.	28 cm = 11 in.
7 cm = 2¾ in.	30 cm = 12 in.
8 cm = 3 in.	35 cm = 14 in.
9 cm = 3½ in.	38 cm = 15 in.
10 cm = 4 in.	40 cm = 16 in.
11 cm = 4½ in.	45 cm = 18 in.
12 cm = 4¾ in.	50 cm = 20 in.
13 cm = 5 in.	60 cm = 24 in.
14 cm = 5½ in.	70 cm = 29 in.

INTRODUCTION

No one knows just how many heathers are planted each year and we would certainly not care to hazard a guess. We do know, however, that a large proportion of these will be selected properly, and grow away into fine plants giving years of pleasure as well as reducing the amount of time taken in keeping the garden looking neat and colourful. What of those plants not as fortunate, put into the wrong soil or in unsuitable situations, not watered properly to start them off and left untrimmed? In the following pages we endeavour to show some of the pitfalls that are to be avoided if success is to be achieved and also to pass on some of the tips we have learned in the years since we first took an interest in these charming, natural plants.

Starting with a brief history and background we pass on to a chapter that describes how plants are named and classified. A little time spent studying this will, we hope, give a better understanding of your heathers. Their garden uses follow together with suggestions for twelve months of colour. Here many will have their own ideas. Use them! For nothing gives greater satisfaction than a garden created for, and by, oneself. We have merely noted down some of the rules that in our own experience have proved to be practical.

However good is the design, the physical side is possibly even more important: correct soil, neither too dry a site nor too wet; plenty of light is essential, demanding a position away from the deep shade of trees and buildings. These are all points taken up in our next chapter. Some suggested colour groupings, then subsequent care of the established plants and the little troubles that can crop up are dealt with. Although heathers do not need a lot of looking after, these cannot be wholly regarded as subjects that thrive on neglect! Peat and its use in the cultivation of heathers is also discussed. Many soils will support this group of plants perfectly well without using this material but its incorporation in the soil not only acts as a conditioner in heavy ground, making it more amenable to cultivation, but also helps retain moisture where it is light and liable to dry out. When used as a mulch there is no finer way of discouraging growth of annual weeds, and of course the heathers benefit too. Sooner or later new plants will be required for replacements and additions to those already growing in the garden. Various ways of increasing stock are dealt with in the chapter on propagation. Cuttings, layering, from divisions and also seed offer alternative methods and the merit of each is described.

Colour section

The purpose of the natural colour photographs is to illustrate the great variation in heathers and their year-round flowering capabilities. Here the publishers have allowed us full scope. Starting with the winter and spring, plants are portrayed both in flower and with coloured foliage. Summer heathers often flower well into the autumn when they are joined by the later types. In the photographs they follow roughly the same sequence. There are shots of individual specimens, both small and large groups and established heather gardens. These are on a wide range of soils both in Britain and overseas and all demonstrate just how attractive mature plantings can be.

The descriptions

To provide a comprehensive list including most of the heathers currently available was the aim. Although it is outside the scope of this book to give but the briefest note on each, sufficient information should be found here to guide the reader on the likely results from his plants. Winter-flowering heathers start the list, followed by others arranged roughly in order of blooming, they are grouped within each species according to flower colour or other similarity rather than in alphabetical order. There is an index of all the plants described in order to find them quickly the list.

The large number of cultivars available can often cause confusion to the novice planter confronted with a seemingly endless amount of names. To assist in making a selection we have marked some of the most outstanding thus †. These are all good, well tried sorts and should be available generally.

In conclusion there are two people to whom we would like to

say a special 'thank you'. Sir John Charrington, who has kindly endorsed the book, has been a source of encouragement over many years both by his recommendations to others to buy their plants from us and also, of course, by his own orders. He was, in fact, our very first customer!

Mr David McClintock, as many will already know, is an eminent writer on botanical subjects. It is our good fortune that he numbers heathers among his favourite plants. We were very pleased therefore when he agreed, although in the throes of completing a book of his own, to read through the rough draft of this for us. When it came back with suggestions pencilled in, many were adopted and we are most grateful to him for his help. We must point out, however, that any inaccuracies in the published text are entirely our responsibility and should any appear these will no doubt be put right in future impressions.

Brian and Valerie Proudley
St Briavels, Gloucestershire

Abbreviations

C.v.   *Calluna vulgaris*
E.   *Erica*
D.   *Daboecia*
cv(s)   Cultivar(s)

For a simple glossary of botanical terms see pages 129–30, following the colour section.

1 HEATHERS – PLANTS FOR TODAY

Although heathers have been grown as garden plants for many years there has never been quite as much interest shown in them previously as there is at the present time. Shall we consider for a moment why this is so? First, the trend today is towards a garden that once planted will require the minimum of attention to keep it looking neat and attractive at all times. Second, the planting needs to be permanent, rendering annual replacements unnecessary. This is where heathers come into their own for, once planted and established, they will cover the ground with a carpet of growth that annual weeds do not penetrate, and on most soils will provide a year-round display from flower and foliage. We must add that we say 'once established', for they have often been included among 'ground-cover plants' which erroneously to many means something to be popped into any odd corner often where little else will grow. It is, however, not quite as easy as that. The weed-covering only comes into effect after the plants have had a few seasons to spread and join together, and are therefore not for the lazy gardener. However, attention to adequate preparation of the site, regular maintenance of the young plants and, most important of all, the careful selection of the varieties to suit the soil, will pay handsome dividends in the years ahead.

Heathers as garden plants have a surprisingly long history. The valuable winter-flowering *Erica carnea* was, according to the Royal Horticultural Society's *Dictionary of Gardening*, introduced into cultivation in this country as long ago as 1763 and the 'Tree heather' *E. arborea*, a native of the warmer parts of Europe and of some of the cooler parts of Africa from the equator northwards, even earlier in 1658. These early records are for plants grown in botanical gardens and private collections of the time, and they probably took many years before appearing in ordinary gardens. The main interest in the last century was in exotic 'Cape heaths' from southern Africa. These were grown in the conservatory and also in specially constructed glasshouses. The rather exacting cultivation of these beautiful plants has led to their virtual disappearance from Britain although a few species and hybrids may be seen in botanic gardens and as pot plants sold by florists during the winter months. As time went along, travellers brought back forms of other species from various parts of Europe to swell the numbers grown in the collections. Our own native heathers, however, have provided the bulk of the garden plants we grow today. Who has not picked bunches of heather and dug up a root or two from a favourite holiday spot? Very often these find their way into the garden as mementoes. Those with deeper-coloured flowers than normal, and others with unusual foliage have eagerly been gathered, and indeed still are. 'Lucky White Heather' is a prize find, as are those with double flowers. Nurserymen took a hand at propagating these finds and also went searching on their own to add to the numbers grown. What surprises us is that, of a list of recommended varieties published in 1900, virtually all are still available today. The introduction of the better-named forms of the winter-flowering *E. carnea* in 1911 went a long way towards changing the image of the heathers from being mere mementoes and curiosities into the fine garden plants as we know them today. Gradually, instead of putting in a plant or two along with other subjects, bigger things were happening, for in 1920 gardeners were being urged to 'plant colonies of heather in beds either with or without rocks' and a few years later, to 'visit mountain and moor to study nature at first hand' – the idea being to return home with a picture in the mind of the magnificent drifts of colour, and be prepared to duplicate the panorama in their gardens complete with great crags, cascading streams and valleys, etc., the whole traversed with sheepwalks of mown heather turf. How many gardens of this type were ever constructed we do not know, but some notable heather gardens were established in the years that followed. The labour-saving possibilities started to become better known after the last war when garden help was so scarce, and today, as well as in heather gardens as such, they are used for filling up beds that formerly held annual bedding plants, for the fronts of shrubberies, under-planting roses, and in window-boxes, as well as in the more traditional rock garden.

A milestone occurred in the world of heathers in the early

1960s when Sir John Charrington, a very keen grower of heathers, originated the idea of forming a society to promote the growing interest in these plants, with exchanges of information and methods. He arranged a meeting in the lecture-room at the R.H.S. New Hall where the idea was enthusiastically received by the group assembled. The Heather Society was formed and each year since then has gone from strength to strength. Interest is world-wide and each member receives a Yearbook filled with the experiences of others on growing heathers under differing conditions. In addition there is a quarterly Bulletin which gives the latest information. The Society has been appointed the World Registration Authority for heather names. Anyone wishing to introduce a new cultivar or variety to cultivation should first of all register the name by applying to the secretary who will ensure that a duplication of names, something that has happened in the past, is avoided and that the name complies with the International Code of Nomenclature. In Holland, too, there is a Society whose speciality is heathers, named Ericultura; its membership at the time of writing is rising steadily, which gives us an indication of the growing interest in that country.

Their ability to contend with differing conditions means that heathers may be seen in gardens in Europe, North America, Japan and New Zealand. Most parts of Britain are fortunate in being able to grow all the species generally referred to as hardy but in northern and central Europe some are unsuitable due to the harsh winters. In the United States, they thrive along the two seaboards, particularly in the north-western States, extending to Northern California, and in the north-east from Maine to Virginia, although many do not stand the test of time here due to the bitter winters and sizzling summers. In New Zealand the discovery of heathers is only in its infancy but as they grow so well over much of the country, many should be planted there in the future.

What of the future? That many exciting new finds will be introduced is certain and there are several undergoing trial at present. Only when proved to be distinct and worthwhile will they be added to the list of many hundred different cultivars available today. As gardens get smaller interest could possibly centre on the compact growing forms, and breeding for specific results has hardly been touched on to date. Fashion in plants, and gardens too, changes very slowly but surely. One thing we feel certain of is that heathers are plants not only for today – but for tomorrow too!

Hardiness

2 THE ORIGINS OF HEATHERS

Heathers – what are they?

Looking at some of the smaller-growing forms of heather it is hard to believe that they are in fact shrubs, but shrubs they are, varying in height in these islands from under 10 cm to over 5 m according to species, and each is evergreen. The wild plants will mostly be found growing in acid soils, heathlands, commons and moors, for the majority are lime-hating, although there are some excellent species that thrive in a moderately alkaline soil. The hardy heathers are native to Europe including the British Isles and also North Africa. Hardy in this sense means that the plants will stand a good deal of frost and wintry weather. Many people use the word 'hardy' to describe a plant capable of withstanding gales or bad soil conditions. This the heathers will do superbly in many instances, but in this case it is not the reason for the use of the adjective.

Where have they come from?

The garden heathers have all been derived initially from one or more of these hardy species. What is a species? According to the dictionary a species is 'A group [of plants in this case] resembling one another in every way and which are capable of reproducing themselves with identical characteristics for generation after generation'. The species is the basic unit in the system of classification that rules not only plants, but the whole of biology and an understanding of the way plants are classified, although not essential to gardening, gives an added dimension. Species with close similarities are grouped together to form a genus (plural genera). Two species of heathers in the same genus are sometimes capable of crossing with one another to form a hybrid plant. A genus may consist of a single species if there are no others similar enough to be included with it. Such is the case with the genus *Calluna* with only one recognized species. On the other hand the genus can be very large. Take *Erica* for instance. This has well over 600 different species, most of which are found only in South Africa. *Calluna, Erica* – these two genera with *Daboecia* making a third, are the plants generally referred to as heathers, and are botanically similar enough to have been included at one time in the genus *Erica*.

So far we have talked of the wild plants and how they are classified but what of the plants grown in gardens? Although we do grow some species, almost all are cultivars or clones. These are terms which have come into use only recently (proposed in 1923 but in general use only in the last decade or so) and are applied to plants which have to be propagated individually and vegetatively. In the botanical sense a variety is a further division of a species, but we gardeners often slip back into the past by describing a plant as a variety when we should be calling it a cultivar or clone. A cultivar or clone is the name applied to a line of identical plants propagated by vegetative means only; each plant is therefore part of the original and will retain its special characteristics. If it sports or mutates, a rare occurrence, the sport or mutation in turn must receive a cultivar or clonal name.

How are they named?

All plants have been given botanical Latin names, and many garden plants have special names too in order for us to differentiate between cultivated plants within the same species. To say a plant's name is in Latin is not strictly correct, for many are Greek in origin and they can be in any language, as long as it can be presented in a Latinized form. People are often commemorated in such a name. Take that pretty little plant Mackay's heath for example. This was found in 1834 in south-west Connemara by a local schoolmaster and his friend and sent to the Curator of the Botanic Garden at Ballsbridge in Dublin. He was a Scot by the name of J. T. Mackay, and thinking it a form of *Erica cinerea* he sent it on to the British Museum for comment. They however decided it to be a 'good' species and it was named *Erica mackaiana* after the introducer. Sometimes the name is descriptive, e.g. *carnea* = flesh coloured (the flowers); or denoting its country of origin, e.g. *lusitanica* = from Portugal; or a distinguishing feature, e.g. *terminalis* = flowers in a terminal cluster.

As for the correct pronunciation of these names this is another matter altogether, for Latin pronunciation not only varies from country to country but even within the country. For example the name for the Dorset heath is *Erica ciliaris*, cilia = an eyelash, referring to the hairs that fringe the foliage. This is traditionally pronounced as silli'ar'is with the emphasis on the middle syllable. In the Reformed Academic Latin this becomes killi'ar'is but a person brought up to speak church Latin will say chilli'ar'is. Which is correct? What each way has in common is how the name is broken up into imaginary syllables depending on its length and the amount of vowels present. Where there would be only two such syllables the stress is placed on the first, but in longer words it comes on the one before the last. Therefore a short name, i.e. *vag*'ans differs from one with more syllables, i.e. ter'min'*al*'is.

Dr W. T. Stearn sums it all up most succinctly in *Botanical Latin* by stating 'It is more important to be understood in conversation than to conform to a standard and be unintelligible.' Many are still under the impression that Latin is unnecessary in this day and age. 'Why not use English names for all plants?' they ask. The trouble with this is the fact that most plants, heathers included, have several names that differ widely in various parts of the country. Also, what of other countries? We call *Erica vagans* 'Cornish heath', but in France it is known as Bruyère vagabonde; and although the average person will not be discussing plants on an international basis, the use of Latin for plant names is far more precise and leads to less confusion. All the same, where a plant has a recognized English name it is quite in order to use it if others can understand. For instance, Dorset heath 'Corfe Castle' can only mean one plant. Irish heath 'Alba' is not so good. Does it mean *Erica erigena* (*mediterranea*) 'Alba' or *Daboecia cantabrica alba*, also sometimes called Irish heath? Let us look at some heather names to see how they are formed. This will tell us quite a lot about their origin.

Erica umbellata

Erica carnea 'Springwood White'

Erica x *darleyensis* 'Darley Dale'

All three start with the name *Erica*. This is the Latin name of the genus and is known as the generic name. The second word denotes the species (the specific epithet) and starts with a small letter. All plant names contain at least these two words which are normally printed in italics. *E. umbellata* is an example of this and is the name of a wild species of the genus *Erica*.

Now notice the names printed in roman type between the single quotes; these always start with a capital letter and are the cultivar or clonal names or as they are sometimes called the fancy names. They are only used for plants brought into cultivation. Our example for this is *Erica carnea* 'Springwood White'.

The third name is for a hybrid. When two plants in the same genus cross to form a hybrid then it is written with an 'x' as in *Erica* x *darleyensis* [*E. carnea* x *E. erigena* (*mediterranea*)]. 'Darley Dale' is the cultivar name of one single seedling of this cross and is only true to name if propagated vegetatively.

As we have already mentioned nearly all the heathers grown in our gardens are cultivars. There are several ways in which cultivars may occur. First and foremost are the colour selections made either from plants occurring in the wild or from cultivated plants. Albino forms of most heathers have been found as well as those with deeper- or paler-coloured flowers or in some cases with completely different colours from the normal. Some may be found with silver or grey foliage due to a greater amount of hairs present and very attractive they can look too. Occasionally a mutant form will arise with double or filled flowers, or perhaps one shoot is produced with brightly-coloured foliage instead of the normal green. Then there are the dwarf forms and geographical variations. All these become cultivars when propagated by vegetative means and brought into cultivation, but some are unstable and revert. Another way a new plant can come about is when two species cross to form a hybrid. The result is usually intermediate between the two parents and the plant often seems to inherit the most desirable points of both, and some of the best heathers have come about in this way. So far it has been nature herself that produced most of the hybrids using bees and other insects or even the wind to do the cross-pollinating. Where the hybrids have occurred in the wild it has taken a keen-eyed person to spot them and introduce them to the garden, where they can be grown on and further increased by cuttings; for left in their native home they will not last for long as there is rarely a place in the wild for such as these.

It is said that over one thousand different cultivars have been named over the years. Several hundred – mostly the better ones – are still available, and more are being added to the list all the time. With all this variety, and the fact that different species flower at each season of the year, it will be seen that a garden filled with various heathers can be full of interest and colour at all times.

planting distances

3 USES

In using heathers as garden plants so much depends on personal tastes, and also the situation where the planting is to take place, that we do not wish to lay down too many hard and fast rules about how it is to be done. We will therefore guide the reader along the lines that we have found the most successful over the years. Let us first of all take spacing, for instance. This is the distance the plants are to be grown from each other. Where one writer will advocate 0·3 m (1 ft), another will say 1 m (3 ft), quite a difference! However, if the planting is for quick ground cover, it is little use planting at the latter spacing for it could take several seasons for the plants to meet up to achieve the desired result, for close planting is nature's way of clothing the soil. Wider spacing means that the individual plants will be of a better shape, for then they develop unhampered and they are easier to prune but cultivation to keep down the weeds is required until they do meet. Here we would suggest a compromise. Try putting the plants in at three per 1 m² (1 sq yd). For quicker cover, move the plants in closer or for the more vigorous-growing cultivars such as *Erica carnea* 'Springwood White' a little wider. The descriptive list should give an idea of the rate of growth for the different species and their cultivars. Three plants per 1 m² (1 sq yd) is the average for most, but *Erica erigena* cultivars need about 0·8 m (2½ ft) between them and 'Tree Heaths' more like 1·5 m (5 ft). It is usually possible to interplant smaller-growing sorts between the tall growers.

Borders and rockeries

Many borders that formerly contained bedding plants are now being planted up with heathers. Here the most common mistake is to have single plants of too wide a range of cultivars and in a great mixture of different colours. Of course the size of the bed will determine the quantity of each, but always bear in mind that the best effect is obtained when there is a mass of one colour, or two or three contrasting colours where space permits; this is far better than a mixture of many different shades. The exact number can vary from as few as three or five up to perhaps fifty of a single kind. Note the odd numbers when small amounts are planted. This is to avoid any sense of formality as when two or four plants are used. The secret in the quantity of each is to get the right balance in relation to other planting. For instance, a border to be viewed from a distance will require larger drifts of each colour rather than one planned to be seen close at hand. Sometimes it is a good idea when dealing with a smallish area to concentrate on a good display for a short period rather than attempt a half-hearted year-round effect. When the flowers fade, attention may then be drawn to a different focal point, where instead of seeing a mixture of a wide range of plants both in and out of flower, a group in perfect colour is to be seen. If on the other hand they are to go on a rockery then the opposite will apply, for this is a feature in which the full twelve months' display is expected and much smaller individual quantities are in order. Even here they should not be dotted about but kept in pockets of one colour. Choose small-growing kinds for preference as they will be more in keeping with the scale, bright-coloured cultivars of *Erica cinerea* – the Bell heath – will look especially well against

[23]

the rugged stone, the small-growing lings, *Calluna* 'Mrs Ronald Gray', 'Foxii Nana', 'Mousehole', etc. will be happy in the crevices and nooks where their roots can penetrate deep under the rocks to search out moisture during a hot spell. The various coloured forms of the Cross-leaved heath will be better lower down the slope where the ground is more level for they do not like a place that gets too dry although the garden forms, unlike the wild plant, do not need bog conditions in which to thrive. We must not forget the Alpine heath either, for this flowers in the depths of winter and will be at its best when little else is out. The early spring-flowering bulbs are most attractive when seen peeping through the heaths when they are smothered in flower, e.g. yellow *Narcissus* with *Erica carnea* 'Ruby Glow', white *E.c.* 'Snow Queen' and tiny *Iris* in shades of blue and yellow. The *Crocus* too look well and make fine companions for the heathers. Where possible choose the small-growing bulbs, for the larger florist's forms of *Narcissus* and tulips are rather out of character. When the flowers fade the foliage is largely hidden by that of the heathers which is an advantage. On a raised rock garden the existing soil is not nearly as important as in other positions such as the open garden, for it is not difficult to prepare a special area for the plants by mixing lime-free loam with peat and coarse grit or sand for those that have gardens with alkaline soil. Should the diet for the plants be rather spartan, then so much the better, for on the rock garden speed of growth is not usually the aim. A feature such as this planted with a wide range of these slow growers will prove an attraction at all times, and even more so if water of some kind can be incorporated in the design to mirror the planting; and of course the water, either a stream or pool, will always provide added interest.

Heather gardens

A heather garden proper can take many forms. Ideally sited in an open sunny position exposed to the natural elements, a bed containing a single cultivar or many, or better still, a series of such beds perhaps linked with a stone path and stepping-stones through the bed to facilitate maintenance where the area is large. A garden seat placed amidst the heathers can be a pleasant place to sit on a warm day when the air is filled with the honey-like fragrance of the plants. Where the beds are in a lawn they are best shaped in an irregular fashion and in no way formal, for it must be borne in mind that heathers give the best effect when grown in a natural manner as though nature herself has taken a hand in the planting.

Where the ground is flat and the area for the planting fairly large, the aim will be to achieve an undulating effect. By planting heathers of varying heights the need for a lot of soil shifting will be avoided. Tree heaths planted either singly or in groups will also provide the extra height, as will a selection of the slower-growing conifers that blend so well with the heathers. In the larger garden other members of the *Ericaceae* (heath family) can also be utilized. *Pernettya* and *Gaultheria* have interesting berries; *Kalmia*, *Andromeda* and *Rhododendron* are planted for their flowers. The smaller species of *Rhododendron* associate better than the large-flowered hybrids. Plant *R*. 'Augfast', 'Yellowhammer', 'Cilipinense' and the like. Dwarf willows, *Potentilla fruticosa* and certain small-growing species of *Rosa* will also serve to provide both a contrast in colour and in habit of growth to the main planting of heathers.

Where space allows and conditions permit, a group of Silver Birch (*Betula pendula*) underplanted with heathers can make an attractive feature. Forms of *Erica* x *darleyensis* and *E. carnea* in particular will be a welcome sight on a winter's day with the flowers contrasting beautifully with the silver trunks. This is one of the few instances where heathers may safely be planted under trees for they do not generally do well in such situations, becoming drawn up and lacking in flower. The birches with their upright habit and tiny leaves do not usually have this effect and allow the sun to filter through to the plants growing beneath. A little word of warning here. After several years when the trees mature, the ground around them can become excessively dry especially in summer and is no longer suitable for underplanting. Any place that dries out completely will require careful consideration before planting. It is surprising just how dry it is at the base of a house wall for instance where often the rain is deflected by the roof. A sunny bank in the open garden is quite different. Although it may become dry in summer, as long as plenty of peat is worked in before planting and the young heathers are watered until established, little trouble will be experienced; in fact usually the opposite will apply for they are sun-lovers and in such a position their roots will penetrate deeply to find the moisture.

Plant the heathers in bold groups of one colour rather than a mixture of many, and in such a way that each is distinct from its neighbour. To give an example of this take three of the finest summer-flowering heaths, purple *Erica cinerea* 'P. S. Patrick'; 'Mrs D. F. Maxwell', a cherry red cultivar of the Cornish heath; and deep pink double *Calluna vulgaris*, 'Peter Sparkes' – all lovely colours but plant them adjacently, and what happens? The colours are too close and the whole effect is lost. Introducing some pale colours such as *E. cinerea* 'Apple Blossom' an unusual off-white shade, which is not impressive on its own, will have the effect of enabling the deeper colours to contrast with one another. The coloured foliage cultivars are also useful for this purpose as are carefully selected dwarf conifers with their contrasting colours, making an excellent foil for the heathers.

We have seen how the tree heaths and other vigorous growers can provide height but what of the smaller garden where these comparative giants will prove too large? A similar effect may be had by scaling down the ultimate size of the mature plants by selecting others with less vigour. For example, instead of a bed with *Erica arborea* 'Alpina' underplanted with *E.* x *darleyensis* 'Arthur Johnson' have *E. erigena* 'Alba' and *E. carnea* 'King George'. The same can apply to any time of the year. For instance the effect of a planting of *Calluna vulgaris* 'County Wicklow' in a small garden is virtually the same as that of a group of *C. vulgaris* 'Elsie Purnell' in a large one.

Other ways of growing heathers

At first sight it would seem a far cry from the rugged mountain-side or windswept moor of their forebears to the comparative comfort of a city window-box. Yet this is a use to which heathers and the winter flowering in particular may be put to good advantage. With most spring-bedding plants, *Myosotis*, Tulips, etc. the display they give, although possibly more spectacular, is much shorter-lived, whereas the heathers can produce flowers the whole winter long ending up with a special show in the spring. Any of the various forms of *Erica carnea* and *E.* x *darleyensis*, also the compact *E. erigena* forms, may be used. We have seen such a container planted with the pure white *E. erigena* 'W. T. Rackliff' contrasting with carmine red *E. carnea* 'Vivellii' and a sprinkling of mixed crocus and bright blue squills – a charming picture that lasts for weeks. The plants are best removed from the boxes after flowering and located in a spare plot of ground for the summer. It may be that no space is available for planting, in which case it is in order to grow them on in pots to be transferred later back to where they are to flower. In either case try to provide them with sunny quarters for the summer to ensure that plenty of buds are produced. Use the general-purpose mix as on page 63 for planting or potting and give pot-grown plants a watering of liquid fertilizer once or twice during the growing period. When the plants get too large for the purpose for which they are intended, they can be planted out permanently and the stock replaced.

Talking about growing heathers in pots brings us to the next point. Have you considered them as pot plants? Not the sort of thing for the house, but for garden decoration. This may be the only way for those that do not have a garden and still wish to grow heathers. People who grow rock plants often use heathers to give a continuing display when their other plants are over, as there are so many kinds that will meet this purpose. Trough gardens, too, will provide a home for many of the smaller-growing varieties. We have even heard of them being used for 'Bonsai', but this is probably going a bit too far!

Interesting flowering hedges may also be formed by using the most vigorous species. We have used *Erica arborea* 'Alpina', *E. erigena* 'Superba' and *E. terminalis* for this purpose as well as *E. vagans* 'Cream', *E.* x *darleyensis* cultivars and others, where a shorter-growing plant is needed. Do you remember the old-fashioned box edging? These compact growers can be used in a similar way to make a border to a drive for instance. Apart from an annual trim at most they will need little attention, are evergreen, and have the added attraction of flowers over a long season.

[27]

For hedges, a single or double row may be planted with the plants spaced at 1 m (3 ft) centres. The double row is better where there is much wind to contend with allowing a similar distance between the plants and 0·5 m (1½ ft) between the rows which are staggered. Place some light twigs around the plants in the same way that herbaceous plants are supported to protect them first of all from the wind and also discourage undue attention from dogs!

Now a word for the ladies. If you have cut sprays from the heather plants in your garden you are not alone, for many do, both for the house and as a different material to be used in flower arranging. At the Reading Flower Show each summer there has for some time been a special class devoted to an arrangement of heathers which always attracts a good entry and the vases are most attractive indeed. The long stems of *Calluna* 'H. E. Beale' and 'J. H. Hamilton' and the coloured foliage of *C.* 'Robert Chapman' in shades of orange and gold are favourites for this sort of thing and *C.* 'Gold Haze' with spikes of white flowers with yellow foliage are often featured.

Dried cut sprays too can be used for indoor decoration and last especially well. The double-flowered cultivars of the ling are best for this, appearing bright for a whole year or more without water. These make pretty little posies for decorating a sideboard or mantelpiece. Should they get a little dusty in time a rinse under the cold-water tap will soon freshen them up and the colours will remain bright until the plants bloom again in the garden.

These then are the main uses for heathers but not all by any means. By now certain points should have emerged from what has been written. First of all they should be treated with due respect and never planted where nothing else will grow. The planting should be out in the open in the sunniest place possible and in almost all cases away from the drips of trees. Wherever possible plant in drifts of one colour, choosing a different cultivar to complement it. Use the slow-growing conifers and other selected plants to add height and interest where space permits and finally, what is probably most important, choose the correct species to suit the soil unless the bed has been specially prepared, a subject that is dealt with more fully in Chapter 5.

'All-the-year-round heathers' – so read the nurserymen's advertisements in the press. There is no catch about this little slogan for the genus *Erica* alone always has one member or another in flower throughout the year and when joined with *Calluna* and *Daboecia*, the numbers actually in flower during the different seasons are even greater. There are of course times in the heather year when colour from flowers alone is rather scarce, but there is always the coloured foliage which makes up for the lack of bloom. Two peaks are reached in the numbers of cultivars in flower at one time. The first is in late winter and early spring, and the other late summer. It is then that the greatest variation in the species is available, and after the peak is reached, the numbers dwindle to a point where the late forms of the one group are overlapped by the early starters in the next to give a complete succession in flowering. To illustrate this better we have in our garden a small bed planted with one of the last of the Alpine heaths *Erica carnea* 'March Seedling' and also a white-flowered *E. erigena* 'W. T. Rackliff'. This latter plant will still be in perfect flower as the *carnea*'s bells are fading. *E. umbellata* joins in next, to be closely followed by that tiny gem with the big ruby-red bells – *Daboecia* 'Seedling No. 3' (when will this get a proper name?). The two months flowering stint of 'Rackliff' (as we call it) is ending as the various summer heathers gradually begin. Starting with the early flowering forms of the Bell heather and Cross-leaved heath, they will carry the display through the summer months until the autumn when the garden devoted to heathers presents a magnificent sight.

Some cultivars offer an extremely long individual season of bloom and many that start in early summer, as well as flowering spasmodically after the first flush is over, will produce a splendid second crop in the autumn. At this time the first of the *E. carnea* cultivars will be ready to open, the buds having formed many weeks before, although some will wait until the shortest day has past, for we are told that it is the lengthening days following a cold period that governs their opening. The buds can be seen in clusters among the stems from early summer, and look so well formed as to give the impression that they will burst open any day. Never make the error one dear old lady did in mistaking them for seedpods and cutting them all off; she enquired of us why her plants had not flowered that winter! There is always the risk that the flowering of this group will be hampered if trimming is done at any time other than immediately after flowering.

The reader will no doubt see from this that with the careful selection of not only the species but early and late forms of each, colour from flowers is possible through the four seasons. There are very few groups of hardy plants that can register such a claim. This does not apply to those counties where snow lies thick on the ground for most of the winter but even here the bells of *Erica carnea* will be developing ready to colour as the spring thaw appears.

A heather in flower each month of the year, twelve months – twelve plants, is it possible? Given similar conditions to that in our own garden in south-west England which is some 200 m above sea-level and subject to fairly cold, wet winters, we can say with confidence that it is. Forgetting for the moment the display provided by the coloured foliage forms which are always attractive there is something in flower no matter what the weather. Come with us now through the seasons – the Heather Year.

Winter

Mid-winter is not the time of year to expect to see much in the garden, but in the heather bed the opposite is true. Here there are several plants in full array. Outstanding among these is *E. carnea* 'King George', a sturdy, tough plant, its flowering stems thickly clustered with deep rose bells, so much flower in fact that it becomes difficult to see that the plant has shiny, deep green foliage. When asked to recommend a good winter heather from which to cut flowering sprays the first we think of is *E. carnea* 'Springwood White'. For someone wanting the quickest ground cover we invariably suggest the same plant. Introduced in 1930 by a lady who found the original growing as a wilding in northern Italy, it was named after her home in Scotland where it was first grown. There are few to compare with this in late winter, with the long, cigar-shaped bells – pure white with ginger anthers hanging down along the length of the stems. There is so much flower in fact, that one could be forgiven for mistaking the plants when in bloom for a bank of snow. Early spring and the winter-flowering heaths are still colourful. One that tends to start off rather shyly in the autumn but surpasses itself at this time of year is *E.* x *darleyensis* 'Furzey'. It is one of a group of tough, free-flowering hybrids whose rosy-purple bells are arranged in strong tapering spikes and, as each bell is furnished with a cluster of dark anthers, the mounded plants take on a deep purple hue when seen in the evening light.

Spring to early summer

Our plant for spring is a new form of the Irish heath. *E. erigena* 'Irish Salmon' is rather taller than our other selections and its outstanding points are good foliage colour and flowers of such a pleasing shade. In fact it matches the freshly cooked appearance of that expensive commodity also called Irish Salmon which we feel Mr McClintock, who found it, had in mind when he named it. *Daboecia* forms are usually regarded as looking their best rather later on, but to follow 'Irish Salmon' we have a real gem belonging to this genus. Named *D.* 'William Buchanan' this carries towards the ends of the short flowering stems good large bells of bright red with a purple sheen. Although this is our plant for late spring we could well have chosen it for autumn as the flowers are carried intermittently for many months, but to us the first flush is the most valuable for it comes at a time of year when colour from heaths is at its lowest ebb. Bell heathers come in a riot of colours – every conceivable shade of red, pink, purple and white, so many favourites that it makes our choice of 'Plant of the Month' for early summer the most difficult. With all this colour to choose from *E. cinerea* 'Alba Minor' would not be the thing for someone who dislikes white flowers or requires rapid ground cover, but if a plant that grows neatly is valued and which at the same time bears a mass of bloom over several weeks, then this will prove a good selection. Although smaller in comparison with many of the other *E. cinerea* cultivars the white bells are extremely numerous and anything they lack in size is made up for in quantity.

Summer to autumn

Walking over the common near her home one evening in 1938 Mrs Underwood of West End, near Woking, saw a sprig of cross-leaved heather that appeared to be very dark in comparison with the others around. Instead of just picking it she managed to secure a stem with a few roots attached. The small twig was taken back to the family's nursery garden and planted. The spot where it went in became overgrown during the war years, and when the ground was eventually cleared several years later the little twig had grown into quite a large bush. Propagated and found to be distinct from others already in cultivation, it was given the name of the finder. Bearing clusters of deep crimson bells amidst grey foliage *E. tetralix* 'Con Underwood' is our mid-summer plant. Cornish heaths too come in various shades of red, pink and white. *E. vagans* 'St Keverne' is a favourite for late summer. The flower spikes are wide at the base and taper towards the tips and are made up of dozens of tiny bells of soft yet bright pink. As well as an Award of Merit bestowed on it by the Royal Horticultural Society in 1914, it received in 1927 the coveted Award of Garden Merit, which is presented only to the very best of garden plants after extensive deliberations. That favourite early autumn heather of days gone by which is still frequently planted *C. vulgaris* 'H. E. Beale' was, in a way, responsible for our next. For *C. vulgaris* 'Peter Sparkes' emanated as a sport on this plant and bears flowers several shades deeper. Producing a wealth of bloom on long sturdy spikes, the individual florets are fully double and are in a delightful shade of clear pink.

Autumn to winter

Our next is also a ling – *C. vulgaris* 'Finale' which displays elegant stems of purple flowers during autumn and, providing the weather at this season remains mild, will continue for many weeks. Mr John Letts found this useful 'between seasons' plant on the Sunningdale Golf Course where it stood out as the only heather still in flower late in the year. *E. carnea* 'Eileen Porter' has in late autumn already been flowering for some time with bells of rich carmine, a colour not seen in other alpine heaths at this time of year. Not the most vigorous of growers, it will none the less gradually build up into a solid compact dome. We are now almost at the end of our twelve months with the heathers and winter is here. Our plant for this season is *E.* x *darleyensis* 'Silberschmelze' whose silver-white bells defy the worst of weathers. We planted a group of these three seasons ago and now they are just touching, although the soil in which they are flourishing was too poor for the roses. The brown buds of *E. carnea* 'King George' that we started with are opening to show that we have come the full circle.

Colour from foliage

So far we have talked of year-round colour from flowers but there is another aspect of heathers to consider and that is the colour display to be gained from coloured foliage. Almost all the species supply us with at least one coloured foliage form, where the colour of the leaves takes pride of place over the flowers. New growth in spring can be bright too and in many cases will outshine the blooms that come later. One thinks of *Calluna* 'Mrs Pat' where the new growth is bright coral red and displayed clearly against the dark green of the mature foliage. Our own *Calluna* 'Sally-Anne Proudley' will lighten up a corner of the heather border during spring when each bright yellow shoot is tipped with red as though an unseen hand has been busy with a tiny paintbrush. A newcomer with creamy yellow juvenile shoots is *Calluna* 'Hugh Nicholson' which furnishes a display almost as colourful as Hugh himself!

The solitary Dorset heath to fall within this category is *Erica ciliaris* 'Aurea' which has such a fragile look about it that one might hesitate to consider it for the open garden. However, the plant is very much tougher than it at first appears, although it will do better in a more sheltered rather than windswept situation. The Cornish heath too has so far produced but a single successful variant with coloured foliage. This is *E. vagans* 'Valerie Proudley' – a white-flowered plant that makes a perfect foil to others with deep-coloured flowers; the foliage is a particularly bright gold after a shower and is valued for both summer and winter colour.

This has recently been given the R.H.S. Award of Merit on two occasions – one for each of the two seasons mentioned, a very rare distinction.

The coloured foliage lings are very numerous. *C. vulgaris* 'Aurea' has been with us for many years. So has the ubiquitous *C.v.* 'Cuprea', sadly rather overshadowed by recent introductions in Britain but still held in esteem both in the United States and New Zealand. *C.v.* 'Serlei Aurea' and lavender-flowered counterpart 'Rosalind' too have stood the test of time, but the really big improvements have come about in recent years with *C.v.* 'Orange Queen', 'Golden Feather', 'Blazeaway', 'Sunset' – how the names portray the colouring! All are due to Mr J. W. Sparkes and his son Peter who together discovered these fascinating plants. Lately they have given us *C.v.* 'Sir John Charrington', 'Spring Torch' and 'Fairy' among others. We must not forget the superb *C.v.* 'Robert Chapman' with golden leaves suffused orange and *C.v.* 'John F. Letts', a prostrate carpeter, is just as bright. So too are *C.v.* 'Wickwar Flame' from Mr George Osmond and *C.v.* 'Gold Flame', which we had as a seedling. All these rival the original introductions. Just the same, we are bound to admit that but for the presence of one or other of Mr Sparkes' plants to provide pollen for bees to transfer, the seedlings that we are now getting would probably not have this colouring.

We have been looking at cultivars for a soil that contains no lime, but what of places where these are not welcome? Here too there are heathers that have brilliant colouring to the leaves and are quite suitable for such soils. *E. carnea* 'Aurea' was the original introduction and still is the first choice for most. For even brighter colour plant *E. carnea* 'Ann Sparkes', although this may take twice the time to cover the same area of bed as the former. A new plant that is rapidly gaining in favour is *E. carnea* 'Foxhollow'. This carries light golden yellow foliage on a quick-growing plant that is also not choosey when it comes to soil. *E. x darleyensis* and its forms are about the toughest of all the heaths and the one with coloured foliage is named after its raiser 'Jack H. Brummage'. More upright than the plants developed from *Erica carnea*, this will prove attractive in or out of flower.

This little survey is only intended as a guide for there are many more plants that can be grown for foliage effect and further details of these is given in the section entitled Descriptions.

A heather calendar

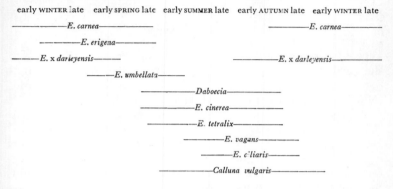

early WINTER late early SPRING late early SUMMER late early AUTUMN late early WINTER late

————————E. carnea————————   ————————E. carnea————————

————————E. erigena————————

————E. x darleyensis————

————————E. x darleyensis————————

————E. umbellata————

————————Daboecia————————

————————E. cinerea————————

————————E. tetralix————————

————————E. vagans————————

————————E. ciliaris————————

————————Calluna vulgaris————————

This calendar is designed to show the flowering range of the principal species of garden heathers. Not all the cultivars of each flower for the full period indicated; and in order to gain the maximum flower both early and late forms should be selected.

5 CULTIVATION REQUIREMENTS

'I like heathers but cannot grow them as my soil is not suitable.' How often have we heard statements like that! More often than not they are based on the fact that a large plant in full flower and vigour has been wrenched from some Scottish hillside, carried around for a few days in the heat of summer, and on returning home the poor plant is retrieved from beneath the suitcases in the car boot and planted, probably already dead. The fact that it has been watered in and still looks alive after a couple of weeks hides this. When it is finally shown to be dead, another reason for its demise has to be found. To quote a well known TV character who states with a suitable country accent, 'The answer lies in the soil'! But does it, always? We know that in the case above, it need not. However, the type of soil will determine the species that may be grown without a lot of special preparation, but will not rule them out altogether.

Heathers thrive in a great variety of soils providing they are neither excessively acid nor solid chalk. Even these extremes can be successfully utilized if sufficient time and energy is available to alter the conditions, as Mr B. G. London did in his High Wycombe garden. Here the house was built on a steep slope and the garden was virtually solid Chiltern chalk. Hard work and determination plus the generous use of peat and leaf-mould paid off as the plants developed and were much admired by all.

Whether in sand, gravel, clay or loam, the heathers will do well but it is the *presence of free lime which will determine which species are to be planted*. Very wet soils will need to be either drained or mounded to allow surplus water to drain off and soils that dry out need plenty of humus in the form of peat or leaf-mould incorporated to retain moisture.

It is most unlikely for soils to be too acid for heathers but many will be too limy to grow all the species without special preparation. The soil may be naturally limy or have had quantities added recently, and before we decide on which to grow we will have to find out whether we have acid, neutral or alkaline (limy) soil, as this has a considerable bearing on what can or cannot succeed. Personally we are not interested in fighting nature over this and if a plant will not do well without a lot of fussing over, we would not waste time with it but rather plant something that will flourish in the existing conditions.

However, this is not the case with all and many do grow heathers in soil that at first would not appear suitable for the calcifuge or lime-hating species. There are two ways of doing this. The first is to replace the existing soil or provide additional material – this is dealt with later. The other is to apply a chemical to the soil. One of the problems of trying to grow plants of a lime-hating nature in limy soils is their inability to absorb iron with the result that they suffer from chlorosis and as a result have an anaemic appearance. The foliage gradually becomes yellowish and often burned at the edges. In extreme cases they do not survive the season of planting and even if iron could be added to the soil, it is quickly leached away without being of benefit to the plants. Fortunately there is now marketed a product that does not have this drawback as its formulation enables the material to remain in the soil for a considerable time. One or two applications are usually sufficient for the season in moderately alkaline conditions. An iron chelate (from Latin – a claw), it is sold under the brand name of Sequestrene. This has enabled many to grow heathers that would normally not survive in such soils. The material is mixed with water and applied to the moist soil around each plant during the spring and early summer. Good results have also been reported when used on acid soils to correct chlorosis that can occur in these conditions.

Acid or alkaline, how do we find out?

The sort of plants already growing on the site will give a clue as to the nature of the soil. Is there wild heather? This will indicate an acid or neutral soil as will the presence of Sheep's Sorrel (*Rumex acetosella*). Azaleas and rhododendrons too favour similar conditions. The presence of Old Man's Beard (*Clematis vitalba*), Beech (*Fagus sylvatica*) and Yew (*Taxus baccata*) are likely to mean that lime is present. A proper soil-test kit will do the job much better than this rather hit or miss method of course. Kits are available at horticultural shops and chemists that will do the job perfectly well for this purpose. A scale has been devised known as the pH scale, numbered from 1–14 which determines the relative acidity or alkalinity of the soil. Taking pH 7 as neutral, figures below this are more acid and higher numbers are progressively more alkaline. A kit will normally contain some test-tubes, distilled water and powder or tablets to precipitate the soil; an indicator and coloured chart completes the equipment. Following the instructions, a small sample of soil is placed in a clean test-tube together with the powder; distilled water is then added and the required amount of indicator; the tube is shaken to mix the contents and placed in a rack and allowed to settle leaving a clear liquid at the top. The colour of this liquid is matched against the chart which is marked with the various pH numbers. Some methods may vary from this, but when the test is complete you should then know just what soil you have to deal with. We would not rely on a single test, but on several taken over the area to get an average opinion of the whole. Remembering what we said earlier, and you find that your test reveals a pH of 7 or lower, then all heathers should do well for this means that it is either neutral or acid. Should the test show pH 7·5 or higher then the soil is alkaline and only the lime-tolerant species should be attempted. The choice is more limited, but includes the winter-flowering *E. carnea* and *E.* x *darleyensis* cultivars with *E. erigena* following on in the spring. Other fairly lime-tolerant species are *E. umbellata* and *E. terminalis*, both of value for colour in early summer. *E. multiflora* flowers in the autumn and winter but is not entirely hardy (although we have no complaints on this score). Where the soil is only slightly alkaline, the cultivars of *E. vagans* may be tried. We have grown excellent plants of this species in a soil of pH 8, with plenty of peat added to it, we hasten to say. The tree heaths too will do where slightly alkaline conditions exist, the soil in this case being not as important as the situation, for wind is the main drawback to their successful cultivation. We will come back to this point a little later. In the case of specimen plants such as these, a special planting hole can be prepared filled with suitable lime-free loam and peat where each plant is to grow. Try to arrange that the level of this prepared site is slightly above that of the surrounding ground and mulch regularly with peat to provide a fresh rooting medium. Be generous with the size of the hole for the plants have to stay there for many years.

Peat

Now supposing you discover your soil does have an alkaline reaction to the test and you particularly wanted to grow heathers for their year-round effect, using both winter- and summer-flowering types. Don't despair! The answer in this case is simply (although somewhat more expensively), a raised bed. For, by raising the plants above the normal soil level, the lime present does not percolate into the peat surrounding the roots as it does normally. Peat blocks formed into a low wall will serve the purpose of holding the planting material and will also be a most attractive feature especially if the wall face is planted up with a selection of the smallest-growing heathers such as *Calluna* 'Mrs Ronald Gray'. There are several forms the bed may take; it may be part of a large scheme where the lime-tolerant heathers are planted in the existing soil and the raised bed takes plants needing prepared conditions. On the other hand it can be a feature in its own right

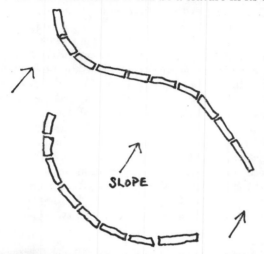

Fig. A   Using peat blocks to buttress a sloping border

and need not be confined to the heathers that dislike lime. The actual shape will be dictated more by the position than anything else, but it could be a circle, rectangle or zigzag. Where the ground slopes slightly a serpentine wall looks attractive and has the advantage that a single wall only requires to be built, whereas on the level the bed will need a wall right around, for unless a large area is to be planted nothing looks worse than a wall with a sharply sloping bed behind it.

The peat blocks are usually dry when delivered and should be prepared for use by soaking very thoroughly. It is no use waiting for the rain to do this job, for if they are bone dry, soaking for several hours is the only real answer. The line the wall is to take is marked out on the prepared site and the soil firmed by treading. Fine peat is used instead of mortar and a thin layer is spread along the line. A single row of blocks is next bedded in, each with a slight backward tilt arranged so the wall will not be perpendicular when completed. Another thin layer of peat goes on the top of these and the next row of blocks put into position, but this time the first one is placed half-way along the block on the bottom row so that none of the joints are opposite one another, rather in the fashion of a brick wall.

The undesirable soil is placed at the back of each row of blocks as building progresses bearing in mind that if the face of the wall is to be planted a suitable medium will have to be provided behind the wall for the heathers to root into. When the desired height is reached the bed is filled with moist peat, or lime-free loam and peat. Allow about 0·5 m (1½ ft) in depth of this material, firm very carefully, taking care to avoid pushing the newly built wall over, for it will be some time before it has settled and the plant roots knit it together, thus holding the wall firmly in place. Level the surface and mulch with peat where loam has been used for the filling, and the bed is ready for planting. Logs make a good alternative to peat blocks. They must be fairly substantial in size in order to allow for sufficient depth of compost.

Soil condition

Ideally the soil should be moist and warm; such conditions usually occur during autumn and spring and this would seem the time for tackling the work. However pot-grown plants are now available for year-round planting and ideal conditions are not nearly so important as when heathers were only sold as dormant, open ground stock. It is certainly more pleasant to plant when the weather is nice, rather than when the ground is cold and sticky. The main consideration is in not treading about all over the bed when it is in this condition after prolonged rain. 'Laying in' the plants is often better. This can be done either in a spare plot or in boxes of peat until better planting conditions prevail. Cold frosty weather is no drawback; neither is dry weather providing copious amounts of water are available for the newly planted stock. The biggest single reason for losses among recently planted heathers is drying out, wind as much as sun being the culprit. So, when it comes to watering always err on the generous side.

Preparation and planting

Regarding the actual preparation of the site: after digging over, be most thorough in removing every bit of perennial weed, for a few minutes spent on making a thorough job of this will save hours of work later on, as well we know the agonies of trying to extricate roots of couch grass and ground elder from the centres of young heathers. If the worst happens and you find you have a crop of unexpected and unwanted guests the next season, hold the young heather gently between the feet when weeding to prevent it being pulled out by mistake. The ground may be left fallow for a time or planted up right away as soon as preparation is completed. In either case a generous layer of peat is spread over the ground to be worked in as planting progresses. Where a large area is to be planted in reasonable soil, we may have to economize here and work in a smaller quantity before planting, and an additional double handful to each plant as it goes in.

When more than two or three different colours are to be planted, it is advisable to work to a rough sketch plan. There is no need to produce an accurate scale drawing for this, as it is only necessary to have something to use as a guide to show the relative position of each cultivar. The information on the sketch is transferred to the ground by marking the position that each group is to occupy by drawing a line on the soil, or better still by placing a bamboo cane with a label bearing the name of the plant in the spot where each is to go. A cane is only needed for each group, but smaller ones can be used for each plant should the planter find it easier to work this way.

Specimen plants, conifers, tree heaths, etc. are the first to go in and having decided on the spacing (remember 0·5 m (1½ ft) average, closer for the slow growers and wider for the more vigorous), starting at the centre of the bed we place the heathers in their positions, one cultivar at a time. Always try to avoid straight lines when doing this and when the first lot of plants is in position, planting can commence. Using a hand trowel, make a generous-sized hole of sufficient depth to take the roots without any doubling over. Work some moist peat in and around the roots and leave the plant with its foliage just resting on the soil. Firm gently. They will probably have to go in slightly deeper than they were grown in the nursery to prevent any swaying about at ground level. When this happens it tends to form a funnel for water at the centre of the plant which will freeze in frosty weather with detrimental results.

Firming in means a light pressing in with the fingers on normal or heavy soil and a careful treading with the feet where it is on the light side. Incidentally this is a job that will also need to be done sometimes where frosts have lifted autumn-planted stock.

Returning to the actual planting, tidy the surface of the bed with your light garden fork and remove the canes when the planting of each cultivar is completed. Gradually work towards the edge of the bed and try to avoid walking on the part that has already been planted. Leave a fairly wide border especially where the bed is set in the lawn, for if the plants are too near the edge they will receive a trimming each time you cut the grass! Do not place too many plants on the ground at one time and be most careful if they are bare-rooted, for there is a great risk in their drying out if they are not got in quickly. Now and again stand back to check the general appearance of your work and do your best to visualize the mature planting. Should you happen to walk on any part that has already been prepared, loosen the soil up again with the fork before planting. Heathers have very fine roots that do not penetrate compressed soil as readily as when it is friable.

Where heathers have been supplied in pots, give them a soaking the evening before they are to be planted out. This will give the water plenty of time to drain through. Peat pots are planted completely beneath the surface and no part should appear above it, even if it is necessary to remove the rim of the pot. Failure to attend to this small point may lead to drying out in a very short time, as the exposed edge draws moisture from the compost surrounding the plant and causes it to evaporate. Clay pots are seldom used these days, but should your plants be in one, tap it out carefully and remove any drainage crocks before planting. Should the roots have penetrated the drainage hole in the base of the pot it is better to break the pot rather than break the roots. Some tree heathers are still grown in this type of container, but the bulk of the heathers will either be open ground plants or in plastic or polythene containers. The ideal plant should be stocky with a large proportion of root in comparison to the top, and these containers hold a surprising amount of compost which enables the heather to produce plenty of roots. Should the roots appear to be matted, loosen the base of the root ball carefully with a sharp-pointed stick. Polythene bag type of pots are better cut open rather than running the risk of damage by shaking the plant out.

As mentioned before, a good watering several hours before planting will always do more good than harm. When the soil also is dry it too should be watered, preferably the day before planting. Always allow the moisture to drain away completely. If it is too difficult to water the whole bed, the plants may be 'puddled in'. In this case the plant is placed in its planting hole which is then filled with water; when this has drained away, planting is completed by working in moist peat and firming slightly. An additional firming will also be required after a few days.

Newly planted heathers will also most certainly need watering. This should be kept up for the first season or at least until well established. Also do not think that watering need only be done after a hot summer's day. There may be a cold drying wind blowing and even spots of rain, yet the soil and the plants remain dry. They will not need flooding under these conditions; a spray over the foliage will suffice. In spite of their diminutive size all the heathers are evergreen and the same advice which applies especially to other newly planted evergreens applies to them, for a lot of moisture can be lost by transpiration through the leaves.

6 SOME SUGGESTED COLOUR GROUPINGS

In the following sketches we endeavour to show some examples of colour selections, which we discussed in Chapter 3. The 'island bed' (Fig. B) is intended to be either cut from an existing lawn or formed as a conversion from some worn out bed. Three variations in recommended cultivars are given for different soil conditions and to give flowers when they are most wanted. The number of plants of each sort will depend on the area to be planted but for this type of feature we consider five plants of each to be the minimum to give a reasonable show of colour. Dwarf conifers are included in this design to provide a change in form and added height. They may be left out of small beds to give more room for the heathers.

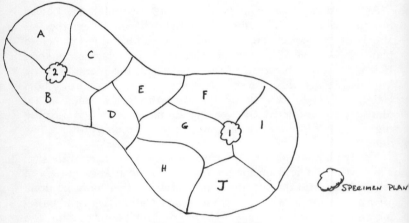

Fig. B   An island bed

The 'rectangular border' (Fig. C) is also provided with three alternative planting schemes: winter and spring flowering for those who garden on alkaline soil – these will do well in any reasonable soil whether it contains lime or not; summer and autumn flowering for a good display over a long period but for lime-free conditions only; lastly, for year-round flowering where there will be something of interest at all times. Again this is also for lime-free situations, but if the bed is raised with a wall of peat blocks which has been filled with acid or neutral soil, it may be sited in any garden.

A third scheme (Fig. D) is a compromise to enable gardeners on alkaline soil to have some summer-flowering heathers by growing them in the raised bed of lime-free soil. The lime-tolerant plants are grown in the surrounding natural soil to which a small quantity of peat has been added. This will possibly be a smaller-sized bed than the others, and here a minimum of three plants of each sort will be in order. In this feature some colour, whether it be from flower or foliage, is present throughout the year.

An island bed planted for winter and spring flowering (any soil)
A. *Erica carnea* 'Prince of Wales'
B. *E. carnea* 'Springwood White'
C. *E. carnea* 'December Red'
D. *E. carnea* 'Myretoun Ruby'
E. *E. carnea* 'Foxhollow Fairy'
F. *E. carnea* 'Vivellii'
G. *E. erigena* 'W. T. Rackliff'
H. *E. carnea* 'Lesley Sparkes'

Specimen dwarf conifers
1. *Chamaecyparis pisifera* 'Boulevard'
2. *Thuja occidentalis* 'Rheingold'

An island bed planted for summer and autumn flowering (acid or neutral soil)
A. *Calluna vulgaris* 'John F. Letts'
B. *Erica vagans* 'Diana Hornibrook'
C. *E. tetralix* 'Pink Star'
D. *C.v.* 'Sunset'
E. *Daboecia cantabrica alba*
F. *E.* x *praegeri* 'Irish Lemon'
G. *C.v.* 'Peter Sparkes'
H. *E. cinerea* 'Pink Foam'
I. *C.v.* 'Beoley Gold'
J. *E. cinerea* 'Coccinea'

Specimen conifers
1. *Juniperus communis* 'Hibernica'
2. *Chamaecyparis thyoides* 'Ericoides'

An island bed planted for year-round flowering (neutral and acid soils)
A. *Erica vagans* 'Valerie Proudley'
B. *E. cinerea* 'Velvet Night'
C. *E. vagans* 'St Keverne'
D. *E. erigena* 'W. T. Rackliff'
E. *E.* x *darleyensis* 'George Rendall'
F. *E. carnea* 'Aurea'
G. *Calluna vulgaris* 'Peter Sparkes'
H. *E.* x *praegeri* 'Irish Lemon'
I. *E. carnea* 'King George'
J. *E. cinerea* 'Pentreath'

Specimen conifers
1. *Taxus baccata* 'Standishii'
2. *Picea glauca* 'Albertiana Conica'

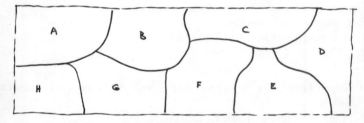

Fig. C   A rectangular heather border

A rectangular heather bed or border for winter and spring flowering (any soil)
A. *Erica erigena* 'W. T. Rackliff'
B. *E.* x *darleyensis* 'A. T. Johnson'
C. *E.* x *darleyensis* 'Jack H. Brummage'
D. *E. carnea* 'December Red'
E. *E. carnea* 'Prince of Wales'
F. *E. carnea* 'Springwood White'
G. *E. carnea* 'Aurea'
H. *E. carnea* 'Ruby Glow'

[46]

*A rectangular heather bed or border for summer and autumn flowering
    (neutral or acid soil)*
A. *Calluna vulgaris* 'Darkness'
B. *Daboecia cantabrica alba*
C. *C.v.* 'Peter Sparkes'
D. *Erica* x *williamsii* 'P. D. Williams'
E. *E. cinerea* 'Cindy'
F. *C.v.* 'Sunset'
G. *C.v.* 'County Wicklow'
H. *C.v.* 'Alba Rigida'

*A rectangular heather bed or border for year-round flowering (neutral or
    acid soil)*
A. *Erica* x *darleyensis* 'Silberschmelze'
B. *Calluna vulgaris* 'Alportii'
C. *E.* x *darleyensis* 'A. T. Johnson'
D. *E. cinerea* 'Pink Ice'

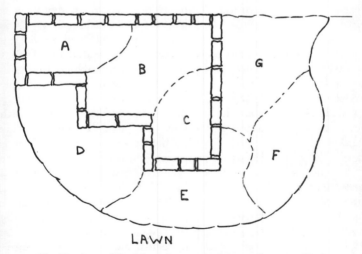

Fig. D   A small bed featuring a raised area using peat blocks

E.   *E. carnea* 'C. M. Beale'
F.   *C.v.* 'Robert Chapman'
G.   *E. carnea* 'Vivellii'
H.   *E. cinerea* 'Coccinea'

A small bed featuring a raised area using peat blocks (any soil)
A.   *Erica vagans* 'St Keverne'
B.   *E. cinerea* 'P. S. Patrick'
C.   *Calluna vulgaris* 'Ruth Sparkes'
D.   *E. carnea* 'Winter Beauty'
E.   *E. carnea* 'Vivellii'
F.   *E. carnea* 'Springwood White'
G.   *E.* x *darleyensis* 'Furzey'

7   SUBSEQUENT CARE

We hope that you did a good job in getting all the perennial weeds out before planting. If not, remove them as they appear and before they can take hold. This applies to annual weeds as well, of course. They may be kept down by hand weeding, hoeing or chemical spray. As this book is intended for readers in different countries we do not feel it advisable to suggest which sprays to use as the brand names will vary. Your local dealer will give advice on which are the best for your purpose. Generous mulching with peat is about the finest way we know of dealing with weeds as they will not germinate and grow through a thick blanket of this material, nor will they grow so readily if seeds should fall on to the surface as most weeds do not care for the acid conditions caused by peat. Mulching may be done with a medium or coarse grade of moist peat, leaf-mould, rotted sawdust, shredded bark or similar material. Be sure the soil is damp before mulching. Mulching will go a long way towards retaining the moisture in the soil during a dry spell. Peat must never be allowed to become completely dry as it is most difficult to restore to its previous moist condition.

Fertilizer is seldom required for young heathers, but sometimes, should it seem desirable to encourage more active growth in older plants, it may be used sparingly. The natural materials are best, as their action is more gentle than inorganic compounds. Dried blood, hoof and horn, bone meal and both liquid and granular seaweed can be used. Sprinkle on the soil before applying the mulch of peat. Fresh farmyard manure must on no account be used as it is far too strong. Even when this is well rotted it is best kept away from heaths and heathers. Apart from weeding and watering there is little to be done in the way of maintenance for the first season after planting.

The next operation we have to consider is pruning or trimming, a subject that many find confusing judging from the amount of queries we receive about it. In actual fact nothing could be more simple. The object is to remove the old flowering stems left from the preceding year and at the same time to keep the plants looking neat. In practice it is the summer- and autumn-flowering sorts that require the most attention, for those that flower during the winter by virtue of their tighter growth seldom, if ever, need much attention.

Trimming to slightly below the old flowering portions of the stem may be done just as the bells fade or in spring before the new growth commences. The latter has much to commend it as the various species can be done at the same time and afterwards the beds can be mulched and generally tidied up. The tools needed are the garden shears or powered trimmer and a pair of secateurs. Trim lightly to shape removing as many of the old flowers as possible without cutting into old wood. When finished they should have a slightly humped or mounded appearance rather than a ball shape. This allows the maximum light to reach all parts of the plant, resulting in even growth and good flower colour. We choose the spring to do this ourselves as we feel that the top growth on some species protects the plants in a severe winter, for such kinds as *E. ciliaris* can look very burnt when they have been cut back the previous autumn. In others, the Cornish heaths for example, the old flowers turn russet and look delightful when lit by the late autumn sun. Such an effect is lost on a pruned plant. Another point to remember is that when tackled in the spring the plants will grow away as soon as trimming has been done.

For the taller plants such as the tree heaths, the secateurs are the tools to use. Just shorten back any long stems to keep the plant in balance. These too can be done at the same time as the rest – just as the flowers are going over. Sometimes these will break or grow out from older wood more readily than most of the smaller growers. In a very severe winter some years back, we had an old plant of *E. arborea* 'Gold Tips' that suffered considerably when its branches were broken by the weight of wet snow. As the plant was clearly beyond repair it was cut back almost to ground level and the branches removed. The stump was left with the intention of removing it at a later date. This job somehow got delayed to the spring and when we finally got around to doing it, we noticed small green shoots growing from the bare trunk. Today it has grown into a strong healthy specimen once more.

Pests

One of the great advantages of growing heathers is their virtual freedom from pests and diseases and in practice little trouble is likely to be experienced with them. The few things we have to consider under this heading are more often than not either rare like the parasitic fungus found on wild heather and seldom in gardens, or little problems such as moles burrowing through a newly planted bed and throwing up their hills over the young plants. Ants too will do this, especially in dry sandy soils. Where a plant is involved in their nest building it will eventually almost disappear under a mound of particles. We have found that if the whole mound is washed away with a garden hose the ants are discouraged and will find another place for their constructions and the plant will recover.

Where moles are involved we can only hope they go away, or where they persist, killing with a spring trap is an efficient way of dealing with them. Although we dislike destroying these otherwise inoffensive little creatures, there is no alternative when we see our hard work being ruined day after day with their burrowing and tunnelling.

Of the parasitic insects, aphids are sometimes encountered.

These are greyish black and appear to us as being the same as those seen on elder shoots in early summer. Symptoms: the first signs of their presence is the curling round of the tender shoots. On closer inspection the undersides of the stem and more particularly the tips will be found to be infested. Remedy: the worse affected of these can be cut off and the whole plant sprayed with a soft soap solution thoroughly wetting all the foliage. This old-fashioned remedy is recommended as some of the newer insecticides can scorch the young growth. Treat in the evening two or three days running and watch out for any manifestations of their return. Apart from the odd caterpillar, this is the only pest we have encountered above the soil surface.

Where new planting has taken place in soil that was previously pasture or grass, the large white grubs of the Chafer Beetles will cause trouble if present. When tiny they do little harm, but the larval stage lasts three to four years and as the grubs grow so do their appetites. At first the finer roots are eaten but eventually the main roots are devoured to such an extent that a small plant will die. Symptoms: plants suddenly wilt and die or look sickly and when pulled by hand they will easily come from the soil due to lack of root. The offending grub is usually found beneath the plant or close by. Remedy: remove grubs when doing initial digging. Dress soils with a B.H.C. preparation according to instructions. Reinfestation is unlikely in an established bed.

Diseases

The one serious disease that is a problem in nurseries, both in Britain and abroad, is *Phytophthora cinnamoni*, a soil-borne fungus which causes death not only to *Ericaceae* but to many other plants as well. It is difficult to identify positively and there appears to be no cure once the plant is infected. Plants die for a variety of other reasons so do not assume you have this disease if you lose one or two. Symptoms: flagging and eventual withering of the young growth in summer is the first sign. The shoots either lose their leaves or they turn brown and remain on the dead growth. In a large established plant a portion will die and it may be several seasons before the whole plant finally succumbs. Death is much quicker in the case of a young plant. Remedy: remove dead and dying plants and destroy them, preferably by burning. Where possible change soil to a good depth. Mild fungicides are of little use and effective types are at present only available for the professional grower. These are considered too dangerous for the amateur and only suitable for cleared ground where no other plants are present. Do not replant heathers in infected soil for four to five years as this disease is very persistent. In Britain it is a problem for nurserymen, but has now, in the case of heathers, been largely overcome. Where clean stock is purchased initially there is little chance of it occurring in the private garden.

Honey Fungus (*Armillaria mellea*). This, possibly one of the most serious of the parasitic fungi, will attack and kill many garden plants but more particularly shrubs and trees. Heathers have been known to be its victims, but it is privet hedges that are most susceptible. It is mainly confined to the underground portions of plants, living usually on a dead tree stump or rotting wood in the soil. Long black threads called rhizomorphs are sent out from the original source which wend their way through the soil seeking living roots of plants to infect. Symptoms: where shrubs or plants die in the vicinity of a heather bed and a heather which was previously in good health starts to drop foliage and turn yellowish this fungus can be suspected. Confirmation of this is by the discovery of the rhizomorphs in the soil around the plant. As the rhizomorphs resemble black bootlaces they have given rise to the common name Bootlace Fungus. Remedy: remove any dead and dying plants. If possible try to locate original source of outbreak. Do you remember a large tree root left buried in the vicinity? Any such stump can be a potential host to this parasite and should always be removed and not just covered over. Remove any Bootlaces from the infected spot. Partial protection can be provided by digging a trench around the bed to isolate it from the surrounding area, but a better way when infestation is severe is to transplant the heathers (if not too large) to a spare piece of ground. The empty bed may now be treated with a suitable fungicide. Such a material is 'Armillatox', a product developed especially to combat this problem. It may be used with safety on established trees, but in the case of smaller plants such as the heathers it is advisable to do this either before planting where rhizomorphs have been spotted, or on the bare soil after plants have been removed.

Marismus androsaceus. Although unlikely to affect plants in good health, this parasitic fungus is known on wild *Calluna vulgaris*. It is only likely to occur in gardens where large old plants of ling have become densely matted and remain wet in the centres. Thin white strands enter the plant usually through a broken branch and attack all parts eventually causing death. When mature, the thin threadlike rhizomorphs turn black and may be observed as a mass wound in and about the lower part of the plant. Remedy: remove affected plants and burn them. Provide good drainage for the soil and space new plants well apart.

Dodder (*Cuscuta epithymum*). This is an annual parasitic plant usually found on heathland, where it forms large patches of leafless reddish stems which twine and clamber over heather and gorse. Gardens that border the natural habitat sometimes have dodder which has started life from seed and sends suckers into the tissues of the plants over which it twines. If left unchecked, the cultivated heather becomes much reduced and stunted. Remedy: remove seedlings as they appear and should the dodder take firm hold cut away affected branches. In spite of its parasitic habit, the writer of these notes has always regarded dodder as a pretty plant especially when the white flowers wreath the heather stems, and well remembers the time – in spite of the fact that many years have elapsed – when attempts were made to try to establish it in a garden, without success!

In country areas animals may be a problem, but the vegetable garden is more likely to be the target than the heather bed. Rabbits are very fond of chewing the tips of heathers, and if only they confined this to the old flowers it would save the trouble of trimming with the shears. Unfortunately they do not have the same gardening sense as you and I, and eat buds and flowers alike. A wire fence right around and under the bed is about the only way of stopping them and one must not forget to inspect it regularly in case of damage, for this will prove to be a battle of wits, and the foe in many cases more determined than you. The same applies to deer of which we have had no experience and

[53]

sheep of which we have. Of all animals, the sheep that are allowed to roam free in the Forest of Dean by virtue of an ancient right must surely be the most determined to eat just what we wish to preserve and will scorn lush grass to nibble and uproot tiny newly planted heathers! Normal hedges are no defence against such determination and at least one local resident has taken to arms (a twelve-bore shotgun) to protect his marigolds, and many's the time we have felt the same, for nothing will incense a gardener more than when his plants are threatened. In town gardens domestic animals can be a nuisance.

8 PEAT

The use of peat in the growing of heathers probably evokes more comment and questions than any other aspect of the subject. How much to use? When? How often? Which type? etc. First of all we have to get one thing straight in our minds regarding the necessity for peat. It is not the presence of peat in the soil, but the absence of lime that is essential to most plants in this group. Providing the soil is lime-free, friable, will hold moisture reasonably well in dry weather yet drains well in wet, then peat will certainly not be essential for their well-being. Where it is heavy and bakes hard in summer or dry and dusty without moisture-holding qualities, then peat will act as a conditioner and retainer of moisture, helping towards successful cultivation. Where soil is only slightly alkaline the incorporation of liberal quantities of peat will give the plants something to root into. The young roots of heathers are very fine and dislike a hard panned soil, so as well as mixing peat with the soil it is a good plan to be generous in the actual planting hole. Now to answer some of the questions we mentioned earlier.

How much to use? This depends on how difficult the soil is but be as generous as the pocket will allow.

When? How often? When the site is being prepared and also when planting is actually taking place. This can be at any time of the year. How often will again depend on the soil itself and the quantity used initially. We also like to mulch the complete bed each spring after trimming the plants. This is simply a variation of the no-digging principle where garden compost is used instead of peat. By using a mulch of peat we provide the right sort of medium for the roots, cut down on the weeding, eliminate the digging (let the worms do this instead!) and of course the beds always have a cared-for look about them. Wild heathers are often seen growing in peat and the flowers show to advantage against this natural background. Mulching need only be done until the plants grow together to form a dense carpet over the ground.

Which type? Peat is formed by dead bog vegetation in an arrested state of decomposition due to the pickling effect of the acid water into which it has sunk. It is mostly composed of sedges or sphagnum moss, sometimes mixed but usually separate. The peat is often cut by machine and stacked to dry – either in the open or in large sheds. Some will be milled and bagged when still slightly moist, and the better grades of sphagnum moss peat are sold in dry compressed bales. Either type is suitable for the heather garden, but for potting the moss peat is best. Always use peat in a moist condition. We make no apologies for repeating this several times in this book, for we have many times seen the poor results from using the dry material. Sedge peat absorbs water more readily than the moss type which will need a thorough soaking. Purchasing a bulk load is the cheapest way to buy and will be delivered loose in the lorry. The drawback is that several tons will have to be purchased and unless used it will take up rather a large space to store. The saving in cost by buying this way will be at least 50 per cent over that delivered in bags. Sedge peat is sometimes very weedy but once the weeds are got out they seldom return. Peat from gravel-pits may contain salt but is satisfactory if allowed to leach in the rain for a season and it would be as well to experiment with a plant or two before putting in too many.

Peat is about the best material you can buy for assisting in growing heathers, but do not think that it is the only thing to use. Correctly made garden compost, spent hops (minus chalk which is sometimes added), bracken (green or composted), shredded bark and rotted sawdust as mulches only, and leaf-mould are all good alternatives. Remember, care must be exercised in the

[55]

gathering of leaf-mould for where the trees are growing in a limy soil the lime will be reflected in the material.

9 PROPAGATION

Raising a stock of heathers is by no means difficult and new plants can be produced for replacements and new plantings in many different ways. Virtually all the plants now being grown in nurseries are raised initially from tiny half-ripe cuttings of the current season's growth taken during the summer months. This is the favourite way of the experienced amateur and professional grower alike and provides a ready means of producing a good constant stock. The modern aids to propagation – mist, heated greenhouse benches, supplementary lighting, etc. – although of great value to the nurseryman having to root several thousands annually, are not a necessity to the gardener wishing to grow a few dozen himself.

Cuttings can of course be taken at any time of the year but some species do not root too readily from the mature wood. Also when very soft the material used for cuttings wilts easily and may prove difficult to handle.

Should only a few plants be required then layering offers an alternative method. Heathers will in fact be found to root naturally where the lower branches rest on the soil.

Division of the plants was formerly used extensively in commercial establishments, but due to the demand for container-grown stock for garden centres this has been superseded by the production of plants raised from cuttings. However, it still offers the novice an easy and reliable way of increasing his stock and old worn-out plants can be used for the purpose.

Cuttings in pots

Rooting cuttings in pots or trays placed in the greenhouse or frame is the most convenient way for the amateur grower. Prepare a compost of fine sphagnum moss peat and clean sharp sand (lime free) in equal proportions. After placing a layer of coarse material – gravel or broken stone – in the base of the container, fill to just below the rim with the compost and firm. Finish off by sprinkling the surface with a thin layer of sand. This will trickle down into the spaces left when the cuttings are put in. Choose non-flowering shoots of the current season's growth when half-ripe in mid-summer or autumn. If side growths are selected, pull them off the plant with a heel of old wood attached. Trim the heel carefully and also remove the soft tip. Ideally a prepared cutting will be about 3 cm (1 in.) long and it should be inserted to half its depth in the compost without removing the lower leaves. A proprietary rooting hormone powder may be used to assist in the rooting, although many do not consider it an advantage, as heathers usually root readily without it. When the pot or seed-tray has been filled with cuttings, it is labelled and either plunged up to the rim to soak or watered very carefully using a can with a fine rose to settle the cuttings in. Subsequent watering should be done with care particularly when the weather turns cool. The glass of the frame or house should be shaded lightly during the hottest part of the summer to minimize the risk of scorching. When the plants have rooted they may be potted up or pricked out into seed-trays, this time using a compost consisting of seven parts lime-free loam, three parts medium-grade moss peat and two parts sharp sand mixed well together. Small plastic, peat or clay pots are normally employed for potting on the young plants which are then given frame protection until the following spring. After hardening off they may be either placed in their permanent positions or lined out for a further period until large enough.

Cuttings without a frame or greenhouse

There are several ways of rooting heather cuttings other than the one described. In fact, we know of at least one nurseryman who, by using the old system, roots his cuttings over the winter period under bell glasses. No heat is required and since these are no longer available from shops, seed-trays with clear plastic covers make a good substitute. A compost similar to that described above is used. Cuttings are dibbed in or a slit is made in the compost with an old kitchen knife. Cuttings of the same length as before are inserted to half their depth, and after gentle firming with the fingers, the tray is watered and the clear dome placed in position. The completed trays are placed in a partly shaded spot out of doors on a bed of weathered ashes or stone chippings for drainage which in turn should be spread over a sheet of polythene as a precaution against worms. After rooting has started to take place, air is admitted by means of the ventilator provided or by propping up one end of the cover. Later when the plants are seen to be growing the covers can be taken off altogether. Cuttings put in during the summer should be well rooted and ready for handling the following spring, when they can be either potted singly or lined out in a nursery bed until the autumn. Young heathers will benefit greatly if some form of shading can be given to protect them from the scorching rays of the sun; they must be kept well watered and at the time of lining out supplied with a liberal amount of peat to ensure a good root-ball for transplanting.

The bottomless box

Some odd pieces of timber, a roll of small mesh chicken wire and a trip to the nearest pine forest with some sacks are all that are needed to construct an excellent device for the rooting of the most difficult of heathers with comparative ease.

A wooden box or frame can be made to any size but for average use something in the region of 1 m long (about 3 ft) and rather less in width should prove large enough and will accommodate not only heathers but conifers and other difficult subjects that do not root too readily.

First, the area is excavated to a depth of roughly 0·5 m (1½ ft). Break up the base of the excavated area with a fork to a good depth and put in a generous amount of coarse gravel or other material to assist with the drainage. Then the bottomless box is lowered into position. Leave the top of the box either flush with the soil or better still slightly above soil level. The box is now filled with the pine or spruce needles gathered from the forest floor. After the needles have been trodden down, water thoroughly. This operation will have to be done two or three times over the next fortnight or so as the needles settle. Complete the firming with a gap of some 10 cm (4 in.) at the top of the box. The next stage is to spread a thick layer of actual rooting medium over the now partly rotted material. A compost of peat and coarse sand mixed 50/50 is used for this and is finished with a thin layer of sand which is all pressed well down. Water this again. By this time the pine needle mixture will have begun the rotting process and the gentle warmth generated provides the bottom heat for the cuttings. Allow to settle before starting to insert the cuttings. These are prepared in the normal way but instead of putting them in thickly they are spaced out so that they can remain in position longer than normal. Treated this way they may often be left until ready to plant out and there is no need to pot them on. The roots penetrate down into the now rotted needles and will be found to have made a fine root system. After the cuttings have been inserted the covering of wire-netting is placed over the edge of the box to provide light shade. If preferred, the netting can be of the plastic type which is easier to cut and handle and attached to a light removable frame. Where the box is sited in a sunny place additional shading will be needed in hot weather. Evergreen conifer branches or green bracken will prove suitable for this purpose. Cuttings can be put in at any time of the year although we have found those taken in late summer are the best and if spaced out as suggested should be in a fit state for transplanting in the following summer or autumn. Watering must be done as required to maintain a humid atmosphere under the shading.

To sum up. This is a first-class method of propagating and depends for success on the points that follow: (1) a good depth of material which must be thoroughly compressed and allowed to settle before inserting cuttings; (2) perfect drainage; (3) adequate shading during hot weather.

Layering

Where only a small quantity of plants is needed then layering of the mature plants *in situ* will prove the most reliable means of increase and is certainly the easiest way for the novice. Many heathers will be found to have formed roots naturally where the lower branches rest on the soil. To take advantage of this, all that is required is for a small amount of soil to be removed and replaced with a trowel-full or so of peat and sand. The selected branch is then pegged down into this mixture by the use of a piece of bent wire or a flat stone. Choose a young vigorous shoot rather than one that is old and woody and leave in position on the parent plant for six months to a year. When it is thought that sufficient root has been formed, the layer can be lifted to check on the amount present in relation to the size of the top growth. Allow to re-establish and make sure there is a good root system before finally severing. Several layers may be put down from a single plant without spoiling its appearance and the well-rooted layers will in most instances be large enough to plant out in their places without the need for further growing-on.

Mound layering and division

As these two ways of increasing stock are so similar they are here treated together. The main difference between them is that in mound-layering the plant remains growing where it is; for division the plant is lifted and replanted at a greater depth. Both methods are employed where a larger amount of young plants are needed than can be obtained from layering in the normal manner. One should bear in mind that one has to sacrifice the plants used for this purpose as they will be of no further use once the rooted layers have been removed. The amount of young plants gained will of course depend on the size of the parent plant chosen. Old worn-out plants are very often utilized for this purpose without detriment to the resulting stock as only the young tips will be retained.

Let us start with our own version of mound-layering. Obtain some flat pieces of wood and nail together to form a square slightly larger than the plant selected for layering. This will need to be of sufficient depth to take the whole plant leaving the tips showing above the top. Place in position over the plant. Now fill the box with a mixture of peat and sand in roughly equal parts, lifting stems and ensuring that the mixture is spread evenly throughout the plant. Firm carefully as you go and when finished the tops of the plant only should appear above the level of the compost. Water and keep moist to encourage young roots to form along the buried portions of the stems. When started in late winter the layers should be ready for planting out after severing the autumn following. The operation is completed by lifting off the box and severing the old plant root at ground level. The young rooted layers are now carefully separated and lined out to grow on for a further period before they are finally bedded out.

Division

A heather being prepared for division is lifted and replaced in a hole that is dug large enough to take almost the entire plant. The centre of the plant is now filled with the peat/sand mixture. Gradually fill in the hole with this and at the same time arrange the stems of the plant around the perimeter. When this operation is complete the tips only will be showing above the soil surface. This is now left for a period up to a year for new roots to form before being lifted. The old plant is now cut away leaving the well-rooted layers for planting out. We once subjected an old plant of *Erica carnea* 'Springwood Pink' to this treatment. The plant had become very straggly due to being planted too closely to a conifer which had developed into something larger than was expected. Instead of discarding the heather it was replanted as described using a barrow-full of compost (it was a large plant!) to fill in among the stems. When lifted sometime later, an enormous quantity of stems were found to have rooted and as a result we finally obtained something like three hundred plants.

From seed

Heathers raise readily from seed which may be collected and sown when ripe. The time for gathering varies according to species but it is generally several weeks or even months from the time the flowers fade. Cutting the sprays when the capsules appear to be ripe and laying them on clean sheets of paper in a warm place will release the seeds. Sowing may take place as soon as they are available or delayed until spring, in which case they are packeted after making a note of the name. Seeds are stored in a cool drawer until dealt with. However, bear in mind that our garden heathers are nearly all cultivars which do not come true from seed although some of the seedlings may resemble the parents. Some of the best new sorts have been raised in this way, but we must confess that nature did the sowing in most instances. Even if the odds of raising something spectacular are long, it is interesting to grow something of your very own and worth the effort if one has the time and patience. Incidentally, always check with as many experts as you can before naming or marketing a plant however distinct it may appear to you. Several introductions have been distributed in the past that were not really as distinct as seemed to the raiser. The Heather Society now records and registers new introductions and is always pleased to assist in cases of doubt.

For seed raising a compost similar to that used for striking cuttings is employed. Try to procure some clay pans of a similar type to those used in growing alpines or failing that fairly large pots in a similar material. After covering the drainage hole with a piece of perforated zinc or broken pot, half fill the container with either sharp grit or other free-draining material. The zinc is to keep out inquisitive earthworms when the pots are later placed out of doors and also helps to stop the compost from washing through. Place prepared compost in next but leave a space at the top of the pot for watering. Sprinkle seeds carefully over the surface and firm. A light covering of clean silver sand is now dusted on just to cover the seed, the pan labelled with the name and date of sowing (for future reference) and watered by immersing to the rim. Ideally the operation takes place in the autumn and after sowing the pots are plunged to the rim in a vacant spot out of doors where the weather does no harm but, in fact, hastens germination in the spring. They can be brought into the greenhouse or frame at that time and potted when large enough to handle, using the suggested mix. Should sowing take place other than in the autumn the pots are best put into a partly shaded place for germination and the initial early growing on. After potting, treat the same as cuttings in the early stages and later line out into nursery rows to await flowering and selection of the best forms.

Composts

Composts are a mixture of different materials blended according to the type of plant that is to be grown. The main ingredients are loam (lime-free in the case of Ericas) peat and sand, together with a small amount of fertilizer to maintain growth while the plant is in the pot. The best type of peat for use in composts is that derived from bogs with a high sphagnum moss content which is usually referred to as 'Moss Peat'; the loam should be sterilized and sifted; the sand must be clean and sharp to provide good drainage. Do not use soft building sand: in fact the opposite is better, for quite coarse grit is suitable for potting. For heathers the following composts should prove satisfactory.

For cuttings and for raising seeds: one part by bulk fine- or medium-grade peat, one part sharp sand or grit.

For potting and growing heathers in pots, window-boxes and other containers: seven parts by bulk loam, three parts medium-grade peat, two parts sharp sand or grit. Heathers will normally grow perfectly well in this mix without the use of a fertilizer but if desired a little hoof and horn (finely powdered), bonemeal or granular seaweed can be incorporated. Do not attempt to speed up the growing process by adding too much in the way of feed, or failures are certain to occur. We find it better to water pot-grown plants once or twice during the summer with a liquid seaweed type of preparation according to the instructions with the product.

The following is a simple compost for growing heathers for a short period: three parts medium-grade moss peat, one part sharp sand; liquid seaweed feed during summer.

1. *Erica australis* 'Riverslea', *E.* x *darleyensis* 'George Rendall' 2 years after planting, in the authors' garden.

2. *E. australis* cultivars, Windsor Great Park, England.

3. *E.* x *darleyensis* 'Silberschmelze', in the heather garden, Wisley, England.

4. *E. erigena*, Windsor Great Park.

5. *E.* x *darleyensis* 'Darley Dale', Windsor Great Park.

6. *E. carnea* cultivars, 'Champs Hill', Pulborough, Sussex, England.

7. *E. erigena* 'Superba'

8. Winter flowering heathers in the Heidetuin, Driebergen-Rijsenburg, Holland.

9. Winter flowering heathers in Wisley Garden.

10. *E. vagans* 'Valerie Proudley'

11. *E. carnea* 'Myretoun Ruby'

12. *E. carnea* 'Snow Queen'

13. *E. carnea* 'Praecox Rubra'

14. *E. carnea* 'King George'

15. *E. carnea* 'Springwood White'

16. *E. australis*, growing wild in south-west Spain.

17. *E.* x *darleyensis* 'Furzey'

18. *E.* x *darleyensis* 'Arthur Johnson'

19. *E. carnea* 'December Red'

20. *Calluna vulgaris* 'Golden Carpet', photographed in winter.

21. *E. carnea* 'March Seedling'

22. *E. carnea* 'Myretoun Ruby'

23. *E. carnea* 'Aurea'

24. *E. carnea* 'Foxhollow'

31. *E. arborea* 'Gold Tips'

32. *E.* x *darleyensis* 'Jack H. Brummage'

33. *C.v.* 'Mrs Pat', showing new spring growth.

34. *E. erigena* 'Irish Salmon'

35. *E. erigena* 'Nana'

36. *E.* x *darleyensis* 'Silberschmelze'

37. *E. carnea* 'Lesley Sparkes', young growth in spring.

38. *E. cinerea* 'Apricot Charm', winter foliage colour.

39. *E.* x *praegeri* 'Irish Lemon', new growth in early spring.

40. *E.* x *praegeri* 'Irish Lemon', in early summer.

41. *E. mackaiana* 'Plena'

42. *C.v.* 'Silver Cloud'

43. *C.v.* 'Golden Rivulet'

44. *E. mackaiana* 'William M'Alla'

45. *E. umbellata*

46. *E. umbellata*

47. *Daboecia* 'William Buchanan'

48. *E. mackaiana* 'Dr Ronald Gray'

49. *E. tetralix* 'Alba Mollis'

50. *E. tetralix* 'Helma'

51. *E. tetralix* 'L.E. Underwood'

52. *E. ciliaris* 'David McClintock'

53. *E. ciliaris* 'Corfe Castle'

54. *E. cinerea* 'Atrosanguinea'

55. *E. cinerea* 'Alba Minor'

56. *E. cinerea* 'Guernsey Lime'

57. *E. cinerea* 'Eden Valley'

58. *E.* x *williamsii* 'P.D. Williams'

59. *E. cinerea* 'Janet'

60. *E. cinerea* 'C.D. Eason'; *C.v.* 'Alba Rigida'

61. *E. cinerea* 'Honeymoon'

62. *E. cinerea* 'Knap Hill Pink'; *C.v.* 'Gold Haze'

63. *E. cinerea* 'Glasnevin Red'

64. *E. cinerea* 'Newick Lilac'

65. *E. cinerea* 'Romiley'

66. *E. cinerea* 'George Osmond'

67. *C.v.* 'Silver Rose'

68. *C.v.* 'Sir John Charrington'

69. *C.v.* 'Kinlochruel'

70. *C.v.* 'County Wicklow'

71: *E. cinerea* 'Startler'

72. *E. cinerea* 'Foxhollow Mahogany'

73. *E. cinerea* 'Constance'

74. *C.v.* 'Alportii'

75. *C.v.* 'Peter Sparkes', 'Champs Hill', Pulborough, Sussex.

76. *C.v.* 'Peter Sparkes'

77. *E. cinerea* 'Sherry' (left); *C.v.* 'Ruth Sparkes' (centre)

78. *C.v.* 'Robert Chapman', 'Foxhollow', Windlesham, Surrey, England.

79. *C.v.* 'Alba Minor'; *E. cinerea* 'C.D. Eason'

80. *C.v.* 'Beoley Gold'

81. *E. cinerea* 'Golden Drop'; *C.v.* 'Silver
Queen', 34, Azalealaan, Boskoop, Holland.

82. *C.v.* 'Golden Feather'; *C.v.* 'Aurea'

83. *C.v.* 'Foxii Nana', Von Gimborn Arboretum, Doorn, Holland.

84. *Daboecia* 'Seedling no. 3'

85. *C.v.* 'Grey Carpet'

86. *C.v.* 'Flore Pleno'

87. *C.v.* 'Tib'

88. *E. cinerea* 'C.D. Eason'; *E. cinerea* 'Pallas', Heidetuin (heather garden), Driebergen-Rijsenburg.

89. Summer-flowering heathers growing in an alkaline soil treated with sequestrene. 'Meadows', Draycote, Rugby, England.

90. *C.v.* 'Multicolor'

91. *C.v.* 'Gold Haze'; *E. cinerea* 'Pallida'

92. Summer flowering heathers in a natural setting.

93. A mixed planting of *Daboecia* cultivars.

94. A heather garden, Seattle, Washington, U.S.A.

95. Massed planting of heathers in a woodland setting. Von Gimborn Arboretum, Doorn.

96. *E. vagans* 'Diana Hornibrook'

97. A heather garden in Northern Ireland.

98. Heathers growing in alkaline soil treated with sequestrene.

99. *C.v.* 'H.E. Beale'

100. *E. cinerea* 'Atrosanguinea'

101. *C.v.* 'Sunset'

102. *C.v.* 'Flore Pleno'; *E. terminalis*

103. Heather bank at Ness Gardens,

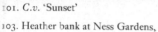

Wirral, Cheshire, England.

104. *C.v.* 'Gold Haze'; *C.v.* 'Silver Queen'

105. *C.v.* 'Humpty Dumpty'

106. *C.v.* 'Andrew Proudley'

107. *C.v.* 'Foxii Nana'

108. *E.* 'Stuartii'

109. *C.v.* 'Mousehole'

110. *E. cinerea* 'My Love'

111. *E. cinerea* 'John Eason'

112. A mixed planting of *Daboecia* cultivars in Windsor Great Park.

113. *C.v.* 'Rosalind'; *E. vagans* 'Lyonesse'

114. *C.v.* 'David Eason'

115. *E. vagans* 'Pyrenees Pink'

116. *C.v.* 'Serlei'

117. *C.v.* 'Mousehole' (left); *E. vagans* 'Mrs D.F. Maxwell' (right)

118. *C.v.* 'Sunset'

119. *E. vagans* 'Cream'; *C.v.* 'Mullion' (left rear)

120. *E. vagans* 'Mrs D.F. Maxwell'; *C.v.* 'H.E. Beale' (rear)

121. *E. cinerea* 'C.D. Eason', E. cinerea 'Guernsey Plum' planted in peat wall.

122. *E.* x *watsonii* 'Dawn'

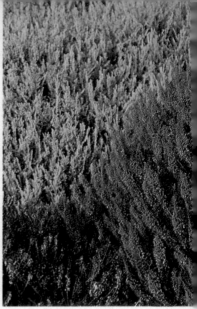

123. *C.v.* 'Barnett Anley' (left); *C.v.*
'Beoley Gold' (right)

124. *C.v.* 'Joy Vanstone' (left); *E. ragans*
'Rubra' (right)

125. *C.v.* 'Darkness'

126. *C.v.* 'Sunset'; *C.v.* 'H.E. Beale'

127. *C.v.* 'Tib' (rear)

128. *C.v.* 'H.E. Beale'

129. *C.v.* 'Elsie Purnell'

130. *C.v.* 'Robert Chapman' (front); *C.v.* 'Darkness' (rear)

131. Autumn flowering heathers.

132. Some double-flowered heathers.

133. *E. ciliaris* 'Globosa'

134. *E. vagans* 'Diana Hornibrook'

135. Summer flowering heathers in Wisley
Garden.

136. *E. vagans* 'Mrs D.F. Maxwell'

137. Summer flowering heathers in Wisley Garden.

138. The heather garden, Windsor Great Park, in late summer. The main display is of *E. vagans* cultivars.

139. *E. vagans* cultivars. 140. Part of heather garden at Wisley.

141. Part of the authors' garden. *E. vagans* 'Valerie Proudley' in foreground.

DESCRIPTIONS

The general description of each species or group is followed by the list of cultivars most likely to be encountered in gardens or nurseries at the time of writing or in the near future. A departure from the usual way of listing is the grouping of plants with similar coloured flowers in each species, and also those that have coloured foliage will be found under the same heading. This is to enable someone requiring a particular colour to find this easily and at the same time to compare it with others that are similar. Species are described in roughly the order of flowering starting with winter and continuing through to the autumn following. Where illustrated, the number of the colour plate is given after the name of the cultivar.

Time of flowering

Time of flowering is the season over which flowers may be expected and will vary slightly in different parts of the world.

Dimensions

Sizes given refer to the approximate size after three years from a usual-sized transplant (one to two years). This will be in normal soil conditions for the species, only to be taken as a rough guide as speed of growth can vary according to climate. Ultimate size will in all cases be greater, often much greater, than the dimensions given, especially so in the tree heaths where over twice the height and several times the spread should be allowed for. Measurements have been taken from growing plants whenever possible. Dimensions are expressed in centimetres (cm). Height is mentioned first followed by spread, i.e. $15 \times 30 =$ height $\times$ spread.

Botanical terms

Botanical terms have been kept to a minimum throughout, except for the following which are used for both accuracy and brevity.
Calyx   Outer part of the flower consisting of the sepals, green in *Erica* and *Daboecia*, coloured in *Calluna*.

Corolla The inner part of the flower, divided to the base in *Calluna* but normally in an urn-shaped tube in *Erica* and *Daboecia*.

Floret An individual small flower, where several are grouped together.

Glaucous Foliage having a bluish appearance.

Inflorescence The whole flowering shoot.

Node The point at which the leaves arise on the stem.

Pedicel The stalk carrying the individual flower or floret.

Raceme An inflorescence in which the flowers are borne on short stalks.

Sessile Stalkless.

Spike An inflorescence in which the flowers are sessile. Often used loosely to describe a raceme.

Stamen The male part of the flower, consisting of the anther and its stalk, the filament.

Stigma Part, usually the top part, of the female portion of the flower, the style, to which the pollen adheres.

Terminal Arising from the top of the stem.

Umbel An inflorescence in which all the flowers arise from the same point at the top of a stem.

Whorled Arising from the same level around the stem.

Soils

Acid Without lime or chalk.

Alkaline (Calcareous) containing lime or chalk.

Neutral Neither acid nor alkaline.

Abbreviations

C.v. *Calluna vulgaris.*

E. *Erica.*

D. *Daboecia.*

cv(s) Cultivar(s).

† Cultivars recommended to form the basis of a collection.

ERICA CARNEA (Alpine heath, Winter heath) (**6**)
Thriving in virtually any type of soil and under adverse conditions, this species must surely be one of the most useful of all winter-flowering plants. The usual wild form has pale flesh pink flowers and is found in mountain areas of south-eastern France, southern Germany, Austria, Switzerland, Yugoslavia and northern Italy. It was introduced into cultivation in Britain as long ago as 1763, but its numerous cultivars show a considerable variation in colouring from the original plant. Flower buds form remarkably early during the summer, and it will be many months before they finally open. They are carried in a dense one-sided raceme and last several weeks, suffering little damage in hard weather even when covered with snow. All are low growing and eminently suited to use as ground cover.

Flowering time: late autumn/ winter, late spring.

Fig. F   A one-sided raceme
(*Erica carnea*)

White-flowered cultivars
'Ada S. Collins' Foliage – dark, shiny green. Flower – abundantly produced on rather stiff branches. New growth is pale yellow like the white forms of *E.* x *darleyensis* which this plant resembles. Flowering – late winter/early spring. Vigorous. *30 × 45*

'Cecilia M. Beale' Foliage – pale green. Flower – large on short spikes held well above the foliage. The first in this section to flower. Flowering – mid-winter/early spring. Compact. *15 × 30*

'Mayfair White' Foliage – rich green. Flower – in short congested spikes. A chance seedling found recently in the Mayfair Nursery, Windham, Pa., USA: named by the owner,

Fig. E   *Erica carnea*

Mr Walter Kolaga. Flowering – late winter/early spring. Compact. *15 × 30*

'Snow Queen' (12) Foliage – deep green. Flower – in dense slightly arching stems, rather stiff growth. Flowering – late winter/early spring. Compact. *20 × 40*

†**'Springwood White'** (15) Foliage – bright green. Flower – large, pure white, each corolla tipped with a bunch of pale-brown anthers. Long spikes on dense trailing growth. Buds are greenish and at first give the impression that the flowers are to be yellow. Flowering – late winter/early spring. Vigorous. *15 × 60*

'White Glow' Foliage – dark green. Flower – silver white in upright sprays. This is reported by Mr Jack Drake to be a sport from the red-flowered (*E. carnea*) 'Ruby Glow' although it resembles the white-flowered forms of *E.* x *darleyensis*. Flowering – late winter/spring. Vigorous. *30 × 45*

Pink, red and purple shades
'Alan Coates' Foliage – mid-green. Flowers – pale rose at first darkening to purple. Flowering – late winter/spring. Compact, slightly spreading. *15 × 30*

'Carnea' Foliage – fresh green-tinged rust in hard weather. Flower – pink becoming reddish-pink in stout spikes. Flowering – late winter/spring. Upright compact habit. *20 × 30*

'C. J. Backhouse' Foliage – dull grey-green. Flower – buds open white with the merest pink blush. Flowering – late winter/spring. Compact. *20 × 30*

†**'December Red'** (19) Foliage – shining deep green. Flower – in strong spikes, pink at first changing to bright rose-red. It is seldom in colour in December and the name February Red, we feel, would be more apt. This outstanding plant was a seedling raised by Mr C. R. Roots, a nurseryman of Pirbright, Surrey, who regarded it as a sort of 'Springwood Pink' and simply called it 'Dark Form'. As it proved to be such a distinct plant it has since become better known under the new name. Flowering – mid-winter/spring. Vigorous. *15 × 45*

'Eileen Porter' Foliage – deep green. Flower – rich carmine rose bells on stiff stems produced over a very long period. Raised by the late J. W. Porter who named it after his wife. Mr Porter was keen on the hybridizing of the different heath species and this unique and beautiful plant could well be the result of such a deliberate cross. Flowering – autumn/winter/spring. Compact. *15 × 20*

'Foxhollow Fairy' Foliage – light green. Flower – on long trailing stems the bells are at first bi-coloured, the calyx pink and the corolla white. As the season advances the whole flower changes to deep pink. Flowering – late winter/spring. Vigorous. *20 × 45*

'Gracilis' Foliage – dull green. Flower – bright pink in short clusters. An old cultivar still grown and although not as spectacular as some of the newer introductions, of value for its early flowering. Flowering – early winter/spring. Compact. *15 × 30*

'Heathwood' Foliage – dark green, bronze purple in winter. Flower – bright rose purple in strong spikes. Habit is upright and bushy. An excellent plant raised by Mr J. Brummage and named after his original home. Flowering – late winter/spring. *20 × 38*

'James Backhouse' Foliage – mid-green. Flower – long light green buds develop into bells of rose. Flowering – late winter/spring. *15 × 25*

†**'King George'** (14) Foliage – dark shining green. Flower – bells of deep rose pink freely produced on short spikes. An old cultivar that still holds its own with the best. Flowering – mid-winter/spring. Compact. *15 × 25*

'Loughrigg' Foliage – mid-green, bronzed in winter. Flower – rose purple bells in good spikes. Regarded by many as a seedling of 'Vivellii' because of many similarities. Flowering – late winter/spring. Moderately vigorous. *20 × 40*

'March Seedling' (21) Foliage – deep green. Flower – shining rose purple, freely borne. We have seen this plant exhibited as 'March(ants) Seedling' and Marchants nursery may well be its source though it does happen to flower during March in Britain. Flowering – late winter/spring. Spreading. Moderately vigorous. *20 × 40*

'Mrs Sam Doncaster' Foliage – glaucous green. Flower – light rose in a long, rather loose raceme. Useful as a contrast to the deeper coloured sorts. Flowering – mid-winter/spring. Vigorous. *15 × 45*

†**'Myretoun Ruby'** (11 and

22) Foliage – very dark green. Flower – reddish-brown buds open to reveal the striking colour of the bells, rich pink at first intensifying to bright red. The individual corollas are of a good size, and the colour is a particularly clear shade making this without doubt one of the finest introductions of recent years. Flowering – late winter/spring. *15 × 30*

'Pink Spangles' Foliage – bright green. Flower – green buds develop into flowers which are bicoloured at first, the corolla pink and calyx cream. On maturity they become deep clear pink. The bells are individually of good size, and the plant is vigorous and spreading. Introduced by Messrs. Treseders of Truro and listed by them as an *E.* x *darleyensis* cultivar. Flowering – mid-winter/spring. *15 × 30*

'Pirbright Rose' Foliage – grey green. Flower – bright rose red as soon as the buds open. This plant was originally mixed with 'Springwood Pink' and 'December Red' and almost certainly the result of a chance seedling propagated along with the others in Roots Nursery at Pirbright. Flowering – early winter/mid-spring. *15 × 30*

'Praecox Rubra' (13) Foliage – dark green. Flower – rather small but plentiful, dark reddish pink. Flowers on a young plant seem to suffer frost damage in cold localities due to their early opening. None the less a good plant to have in spite of this. Flowering – early winter/spring. Compact, slightly spreading. *15 × 30*

'Prince of Wales' Foliage – light green often tipped red. Flower – light shell pink in short clustered spikes. Rather slow, it may be some time before a large plant is formed. Flowering – mid-winter/spring. *15 × 25*

'Queen Mary' Foliage – light green. Flower – clear pink in short spikes. Another old Backhouse cultivar sometimes still listed, it has the reputation of not growing well on some soils, although we have not experienced this. Flowering – late autumn/winter. Compact. *15 × 25*

'Queen of Spain' Foliage – pale green. Flower – light pink, tinged red. One of a group of cultivars introduced by Messrs. Backhouse of York in 1911 to celebrate the Coronation, and often referred to as the 'Royal Family'. This one has been largely superseded by the newer forms but is a pretty plant all the same. Flowering – mid-winter/spring. Compact rather spreading. *15 × 25*

'Ruby Glow' (25) Foliage – dark green. Flower – brown buds, the name gives a clue to the colour of the flowers for they are as red as any ruby. Flowers well and often starts into growth before they have time to fade. Flowering – late winter/spring. Vigorous, spreading. *15 × 35*

'Sherwoodii' ('Sherwood's Creeping', 'Sherwood Early Red') Foliage – light green. Flower – large green buds develop into pale rose bells borne on short but dense stems. Raised in America at Sherwood Nursery, Oregon, the name suggests that the plant develops a deeper colour there. We have grown it here and although a pleasing colour it is certainly not red. Flowering – mid-winter/spring. Compact. *15 × 30*

'Springwood Pink' Foliage – mid-green. Flower – white at first changing to clear pink later. A justly popular plant that shared the same home as 'Springwood White' and is so similar that in many respects the raiser's supposition

that it was a seedling from this plant is most likely correct. Flowering – late winter/spring. Vigorous, spreading. *15 × 50*

'Thomas Kingscote' Foliage – pale green. Flower – light slate pink tipped with conspicuous red anthers. Rather slow growing this is another of those plants of value for contrasting with the brighter colours. Flowering – mid-winter/spring. Compact. *15 × 25*

'Vivellii' Foliage – dark green turning intensely bronze during the winter. Flower – deep carmine red on strong stiff spikes. New growth is rather pretty too. A superb plant that we would not like to be without. Flowering – late winter/early spring. Compact. *15 × 30*

'Winter Beauty' Foliage – dark green. Flower – bright rose in small closely packed sprays. The true plant is earlier, not so robust, more open in growth and not nearly as common as *E. carnea* 'King George' with which it is often confused. Flowering – early winter/late winter. Spreading, rather slow. *15 × 30*

Coloured foliage

'Aurea' (23) Foliage – light lime-green or pale yellow in summer becomes yellow-gold in winter with orange tints. Flower – deep pink in short racemes. Flowering mid-winter/spring. Bushy, rather upright and spreading. *15 × 35*

'Ann Sparkes' Foliage – yellow-orange, old gold later with purple-bronze leaf margins. Flower – rich purple, rather sparse. Flowering – late winter/early spring. A sport from *E. carnea* 'Vivellii' in the nursery of Mr J. W. Sparkes. This has been grown as 'Vivellii Aurea' on the Continent. Slow growing, spreading, eventually fairly large. *15 × 20*

†**'Foxhollow'** (24) Foliage – light yellow-green, becomes rich yellow in winter. During hard weather assumes a reddish flush. Flower – white bells on opening slowly change to pale pink. On closer inspection the flowers will be seen to be two shades of pink. A seedling found in the Foxhollow Gardens in Surrey, it is regarded by many as the finest in this section for coloured winter foliage effect. Flowering – late winter/early spring. Low, vigorous and spreading.

'Lesley Sparkes' (37) Foliage – new growth cream or pale yellow with salmon tips. Summer foliage colour is pale lime. Flower – few, deep pink in short crowded spikes. Flowering – winter/early spring. Compact, very slow. Said to be a sport on 'King George'.

'Sunshine Rambler' Foliage – bright clear yellow throughout the year. Flower – clear pink. Flowering – winter/early spring. Rapid spreader. A recent introduction from Mr Rawinsky of Primrose Hill Nursery, Haslemere, Surrey.

ERICA x DARLEYENSIS
(winter-flowering hybrids)

This group of heathers is the result of marriages between *E. carnea* and *E. erigena*. They have happily inherited the good points of both parents, namely the long flowering and bright colours of the former, and the quick growth and floriferous nature of the latter. As regards height they are midway between the almost prostrate *E. carnea* and the upright *E. erigena*. Extremely hardy, they thrive in the worst of soils and flowering can be said to cover the whole of the winter period until late into the spring. Pruning consists of the lightest of all trimming and then only when needed.

Cultivars with white flowers

†‘**Silberschmelze**’ (**3 and 36**) (‘Molten Silver’) Foliage – deep, glossy green. Flower – silver white with brown anthers carried in good strong spikes. Plant, neatly rounded. Flowering can extend from early autumn until late spring. In fact, as these notes are being written in late May a group of these are still in perfect flower here, in our garden. *30 × 45*

Many white-flowered hybrids have been introduced under a variety of names such as *alba*: ‘Silver Beads’; ‘Silver Bells’; ‘Silver Mist’; ‘Silver Star’; ‘White form’, etc. From the garden point of view they all appear identical with the original pre-war German sport described above. The only exception could possibly be ‘N. R. Webster’ (‘Knockomie’), a seedling found in Scotland, which even an expert would have the greatest difficulty in telling apart from ‘Silberschmelze’.

Pink, red and purple shades

†‘**Arthur Johnson**’ (**18**) Foliage – light green. Flower – bright mauve-pink in very long spikes. This feature makes the plant of use for cutting for the house as well as garden decoration. A justly popular heath it was raised by the late A. T. Johnson who considered it a cross between *E. carnea* ‘Ruby Glow’ and *E. erigena* ‘Hibernica’.

‘**Darley Dale**’ (**5**) Foliage – deep green. Flower – pale lilac-rose becoming deeper towards the end of the season. Vigorous, bushy and ideal for ground cover in the most difficult positions that anyone would wish to plant heathers. This was for long the original hybrid of this group and is still generally known as ‘darleyensis’. *40 × 50*

‘**Furzey**’ (**17**) Foliage – dark green – even darker in winter. Flower – dark rose-purple bells in strong spikes. One of the richest colours to be obtained in this group. Originating in Furzey Gardens, New Forest, it appears to be the same as ‘Cherry Stevens’ sometimes seen listed. *30 × 40*

‘**George Rendall**’ (**1**) Foliage – fresh green, tipped red in winter. New growth in spring tipped yellow and pink. Flower – lilac-pink in dense tapering spikes. Compact. This has always been a personal favourite due to its long flowering and reliability in putting on a good display no matter what the weather. *30 × 40*

'Ghost Hills' Foliage – bright green. Flower – short spikes crowded with deep rose bells, becoming red at times. The first flowers invariably open during the autumn, then, after a short lull, provide another generous display during the spring. Originated as a sport on 'Darley Dale' in Heathwood Nursery, Taverham, Norfolk. *40 × 50*

'James Smith' Foliage – mid to deep green. Flower – mauve pink in solid spikes. More open in growth than 'Darley Dale', yet not as tall as 'Arthur Johnson'. *40 × 45*

'Jenny Porter' Foliage – pale green, tipped white. Flower – virtually white but having a feint blush of pink, anthers violet. Strong, upright, possibly the tallest of the winter-flowering hybrids. See note under 'J. W. Porter'. *50 × 40*

'J. W. Porter' Foliage – very dark green, new growth red and cream. Flower – bright purple-pink in good spikes but not until plant has had time to establish. Habit, neatly rounded, more upright than spreading. This cultivar together with 'Jenny Porter' and 'Margaret Porter' was

sent to the Foxhollow Gardens at Windlesham, Surrey, by Mrs Eileen Porter from her home at Carryduff, near Belfast. They were raised by her late husband, J. W. Porter, and were perhaps the results of deliberate crosses he made, although unfortunately his records have been lost. *30 × 40*

'Margaret Porter' Foliage – shining green, new growth tipped cream. Flower – clear rose in short curving spikes. Semi-prostrate and wide spreading. *25 × 45*

Coloured foliage
'Jack H. Brummage' (**32**) Foliage – summer colour is light yellow, turns golden-green or clear gold in winter depending on situation which should be in full sun for best coloration. In cold weather red tints can also be observed. New growth is light yellow and pink. Flower – deep pink, in short spikes. We find that neatly rounded specimens are easily produced with an annual light trimming. *30 × 40*

ERICA UMBELLATA (Umbel or Portuguese heath) (**45 and 46**)
From the northern tip of Morocco, south-west Spain and

the Atlantic coast of Portugal comes this small shrubby heath. One cannot consider it to be entirely hardy over the whole of Britain, although in the south-west of England we have yet to lose a plant due to hard weather. In its native haunts, although flowering time varies, it may often be seen blooming in winter, but here, late spring and early summer are the rule.

Fig. G   *Erica umbellata*

This is another of those species that may be grown in an alkaline soil as it is completely tolerant of these conditions. However, in the garden as in nature, peaty soils seem to be preferred. Drainage is rather important as it will not stand waterlogged ground, in fact the opposite is best. A position that gets full sun, is sharply drained, where the wood will

get fully ripe before winter sets in, will result in more flower and of a better colour. Various shades of pink and also white have been reported but we have only come across the typical plant both in the wild and in cultivation. Plants may be trimmed lightly to shape after flowering if desired.

Foliage – grey-green, brighter green when mature. Flower – rose-pink in umbels, corolla almost round with conspicuous black anthers. Plant is delicate in appearance, open growing with rather sparse foliage. *25 × 40*

ERICA ERIGENA (MEDI-TERRANEA) (Irish heath, Spring heath) (4)

A valuable group of plants at their best during the spring period when they follow on from the *E.* x *darleyensis* cultivars. They are generally much taller growing than these, and although tolerating the same wide range of soils, including lime, they cannot be regarded as being as totally hardy as are their smaller-growing cousins. However, when planted in groups for mutual protection they come through most winters with little harm. In sheltered gardens they are useful for growing as specimens among the lower more prostrate types. Snow causes the most damage due to the brittle nature of the branches; this is particularly true of the taller cultivars. To remedy this, plants may be tied loosely when heavy snow is expected. Only the lightest pruning is required with this group – as soon as the flowers fade. When in full flower, the bushes are a wonderful sight completely smothered in bloom. The bells are delightfully scented with a honey-like fragrance that fills the air for a considerable distance. Even out of flower the foliage too is scented and is especially noticeable after a gentle rain.

The species is native to Spain, rare in south-west France but relatively common in localized areas in western Ireland where it may be seen growing to the very edge of the sea loughs. This makes nonsense of its long familiar Latin name (*mediterranea*) which means, in fact, 'inland' not 'mediterranean' and which is now known rightly to apply to *E. carnea*. For a time recently *E. mediterranea* was known as *E. hibernica*; this too proved incorrect and in 1965 a new

name was proposed, *E. erigena* (from Erin or Ireland). This would seem to us to be the most acceptable as well as being correct, for the wild plant is more plentiful in Ireland than elsewhere, and as far as can be surmised most, if not all, our garden forms had their origins there. Many produce the odd flower during the autumn but the main flowering time is from late winter to late spring.

Fig. H   *Erica erigena*

Cultivars with white flowers
'Alba' Foliage – light yellow-green. Flower – pure white with pale-brown anthers, borne on long upright stems. Very free. Plant is tall, bushy, makes a fine specimen. *60 × 30*

'Nana Alba' Foliage – pale green. Flower – white, freely produced. Open growth with flowering stems of differing lengths which gives the plant a spiky appearance. *40 × 25*

†**'W. T. Rackliff'** (29) Foliage – rich green, new growth paler. Flower – large white bells with characteristic protruding brown anthers, borne in short crowded spikes. The flowers are so profuse as to completely cover the bush each spring. With us they often bloom the preceding autumn too. Growth is neat, rounded. *30 × 35*

Pink and purple shades

†**'Brightness'** Foliage – grey-green, becomes purplish in winter. Flower – bright purple-pink from dark-brown buds. Habit is neat, upright, elliptical in shape. *50 × 30*

'Coccinea' Similar to 'Brightness' but flowers are deep clear pink with less purple. The true plant is slightly taller and more open in habit of growth. Considered a garden seedling and often confused with the better known 'Brightness'. *60 × 25*

'Glauca' Foliage – light grey-green. Flower – white flushed palest pink. Dense,

upright. Of value as a contrast in foliage colour. *60 × 30*

'Irish Salmon' (34) Foliage – light grey with reddish tinge to new stems. Flower – clear pink with no trace of purple. It gets its name from the rich dark salmon buds which are as much a feature of this plant as are the contrasting pale open flowers. A very distinct colour break. Found by Mr David McClintock by Lough Carramore in Co. Mayo, western Ireland in 1967. *50 × 23*

'Nana' (35) Foliage – pale green, rather dull. Flower – light rose, usually rather sparse. Very compact and of value as a small specimen bush, perhaps better on the rock garden. *45 × 30*

'Rosslare' Foliage – dull, dark green. Flower – light purple-pink in abundance. Upright, fairly dense, this plant has its origins in New Zealand where it is one of the most popular of the hardy heaths. Sometimes listed there as an *E.* x *darleyensis* cross. *50 × 23*

'Superba' (7) Foliage – mid-green. Rose-pink bells flushed pale purple with dark-purple anthers. Upright, fairly dense. This is the tallest of the section producing a splendid display over a long season. Recommended as a specimen plant for bold groups in the larger heather garden; it is sometimes used as a hedge. *70 × 30*

In 1968 the Heather Society mounted an expedition to western Ireland to look for new forms of this species as well as to record its distribution there. The group which was based at Rosturk Castle in Co. Mayo returned with several distinct plants. These have now been propagated and three have been selected as being suitable for garden use and should find their way into nurseries in the near future. At present they are unnamed, the first is bright purple-pink and grows in a very vigorous manner. Another, almost white with exceptionally long flower spikes. The last is a real gem; dark green – almost black foliage, orange buds and slate-pink flowers.

TREE HEATHERS

These giant heaths – by heather standards – are found mostly in Spain and Portugal although *Erica arborea* also grows in Africa as well as around the Mediterranean. They are of varying hardiness, the species already mentioned being the least hardy in Britain. In the garden some protection is advised for the first winter where the planting is at all exposed. Evergreen branches or hessian supported by bamboo canes may be utilized. When planted in small groups they provide mutual protection while the young plants grow to maturity.

E. australis is the most susceptible to damage from high wind and snow. In fact, even where the plants grow wild there is much such damage in evidence. However, if they are planted quite closely, say at the normal distance recommended for the smaller heathers, and provided snow is removed before permanent damage is caused, they will grow together to form a small thicket. Five plants put in closely should prove sufficient for this method and it will be found that each slender stem acts as a support for its neighbour. Alternatively, they may be grown either against a wall, or strongly staked. In the case of the other species it is advisable to shorten back growth by roughly a third each season for the first two or three years or until a thick stem has formed. A cane used as a stake to each plant will be a help in preventing too much swaying in windy weather, as movement of the roots stops the plant from getting established with a risk of failure later. We have grown all these species in a moderately alkaline soil although the best specimens are to be seen where the soil is neutral or acid. All flower during late winter and spring (sometimes to early summer). Ultimate height varies accordto position. Allow approximately three times the dimensions given.

ERICA ARBOREA (Tree heath)

Foliage – pale green. Flower – masses of small ashen-white bells. Fragrant, some say of hawthorn – others, of cats! Buds are formed early and can be damaged by frost in cold areas. Plant – tall, many stemmed. In its natural habitat younger plants give the better display. *95 × 45*

'Alpina' (30) Foliage – deep green, in long plumose branches. Flower – pure white, generously produced. Growth is dense and habit more upright than that of the species and it is considerably more hardy. Collected in 1872 from the Cuenca Mountains in central Spain where it was found wild and subsequently named. The name *alpina* does not mean that a plant comes from the Alps, but from a high place, as indeed this did. *95 × 45*

'Gold Tips' (31) Foliage – new growth pale golden-yellow, tipped deep orange. Becomes bright green on maturity. Flower – light grey, dark anthers; scented as *E. arborea*. Similar to the type except for the superb spring foliage effect.

ERICA AUSTRALIS (Spanish heath, Southern tree heath) (2 and 16)

Occurs naturally in Portugal and south-west Spain where, during the winter months, whole hillsides are transformed into a deep red haze only broken here and there by the white mounds of *E. arborea* and bright yellow gorse. On closer inspection colours ranging from dark red to almost white may be found. Although many fine plants are in cultivation including a beautiful white form, we believe we have been able to increase the colour range available. From near the almost forgotten Moorish village of Castellar de la Frontera, perched high up on a crag in Andalucia we found two others. They are at present on trial here to see if they measure up to expectations regarding hardiness, etc. If they do they will be known as 'Castellar Blush' and 'Castellar Garnet'. The names should convey the flower colour.

Foliage – deep green. Flower – pale mauve-pink in dense, long sprays on previous years growth. Growth, upright – rather weak. Support until well established or grow as described in the general notes on Tree heaths. The cultivar 'Rosea' appears to us as the same as the plant described. *95 × 30*

'Mr Robert' (**28**) Foliage – pale, fresh green. Flower – large pure white bells, golden anthers. Upright habit. Reputedly less hardy than others in this group but fortunately this has not proved so with us. A magnificent plant when in flower, it was named after the finder Lt. Robert Williams, who was affectionately known by the staff of the Williams family as 'Mr Robert'. *95 × 30*

'Riverslea' (**1**) An extremely good form with flowers of a deeper colour than the type. Foliage is rather more glaucous. A seedling found at Pritchards former Riverslea Nursery, Christchurch, Hampshire. *95 × 30*

ERICA LUSITANICA
(Spanish heath, Portuguese heath) (**27**)

Another beautiful large-growing plant with a long season of flowering, depending on the situation where it is planted and the severity of the weather. We have recorded this in bloom in early autumn and still out the following spring and early summer. In the wild it seems to favour the dry barren hillsides, and in cultivation too it will be able to withstand a considerable amount of drought (once established) and still look fresh. Flowers are slightly scented but not nearly as strongly as in some of the other species. May be seen in florists as a cut flower; also, together with the white ling (*Calluna vulgaris alba* and other white cultivars) forms the bulk of the 'Lucky White Heather' sold mainly to expatriate Scots as a memento of home. It has become naturalized over parts of Cornwall and Dorset, reproducing itself from seed, and can also be met with growing wild in quantity in large areas in the North Island, New Zealand, where it is now probably more common than in its countries of origin.

Foliage – light fresh green, soft to the touch. Flower – pure white, cylindrical in shape produced from deep-red buds. Habit, upright and well furnished from the base. Ends of branches often stained red-rust during the winter. 95 × 45

ERICA x VEITCHII 'Exeter'

Originally a chance seedling found in Veitch's Nursery, Exeter. This has proved to be the only hybrid found anywhere between *E. arborea* and *E. lusitanica*. From the garden point of view it is closer in appearance to *E. arborea*, but fortunately, hardier than that species. The white bells are sweetly scented and, although small, the flowers are borne in such profusion that the branches

Fig. I Tree heath *Erica* x *veitchii* 'Exeter'

appear to be weighted down with snow. *80 × 45*

ERICA SCOPARIA (Besom heath)

A tall-growing shrub found growing mostly in the South of France, Spain and north Africa. We have often come across this on our holidays in those areas, growing on commons and in woods in France and mixed with other tree heaths in Spain. The species is seldom planted in Britain although a small-growing cultivar is occasionally. Both have light apple-green foliage that darkens on maturity. The flowers are produced on the previous seasons wood and as they are greenish in colour do not show up well. Plants would certainly not be worth growing for any floral display. Old specimens of *E. scoparia* can be as high as 3 m but are usually seen at half of that.

The branches are cut for use in besom brooms which are sometimes to be seen in shops; on the Continent they are used for thatching barns, hurdles, etc., and we have seen shelters in camp sites effectively roofed with a covering of this.

'Compacta' ('Minima', 'Nana', etc.). For use only as a contrast in colour or as a small specimen in the heather garden. Forms a round ball of fresh green foliage up to 0·5 m (18 in.) high. Although generally lime-free conditions are suggested we have grown this successfully in a soil of pH 8·5 with plenty of peat.

'Lionel Woolner' (26) Foliage – bright glossy green. Flowers – dusky-red in short spikes. Apart from the dwarf form the besom heath has, until now, been regarded as too coarse for the garden and the flowers too uninteresting to be included along with others in a collection of heathers. A new plant has come along to

change that image! Holidaying in Tenerife, Canary Islands, Mr and Mrs Woolner came across a group of *E. scoparia* growing at over 1000 m in the Mercedes Mountains with foliage of a yellowish hue. Some seedlings were selected for their foliage colour and brought back to be planted in the Woolner's Devon garden. All but one soon turned deep green and the following year produced flowers worthy enough to make nonsense of the usual description of the type plant, in that the flowers are larger and more brightly coloured. The finest plant has now been propagated and given a cultivar name. So far the plants have come through each winter unscathed. The single remaining golden foliage form has become an 'upright shapely plant with leaves of a sunny golden-green and has so far produced no flowers.' *45 × 30*

ERICA CINEREA (Bell heath, Bell heather)
This is the native plant that changes our drier commons and moors to a sea of purple each summer. These flowers will later turn russet and when walked through emit a rattling

sound. Is this the reason for the common name? Probably not, but one could well imagine the sound of hundreds of tiny bells ringing. From these purple plants literally dozens of colour variations have been evolved, ranging in colour from pure white to deepest maroon, several with brightly coloured foliage have also been selected.

Preferring a position on the dry side – or at least a well-drained soil, the various cultivars will put on a wonderful show from early summer until late in the autumn. The foliage is fine and varies in colour from apple green and dark green in the white- and pale-coloured forms, grey-green or almost purple in the deeper shades and also gold.

Flowers are ovoid in shape and carried in a long raceme in a vigorous growing cultivar; smaller types produce flowers in shorter clusters which do not require the same trimming as do those with the longer spikes. The latter should be pruned to just below the old flowers in spring just before growth commences.

This group is not suitable for any but neutral or acid soil as they will not stand lime in any

form. Plant in full sun with plenty of moist peat dug in well if the site is likely to become at all dry. All flower from early summer until the autumn, the blooms coming along in several flushes, reaching a peak of perfection on at least two occasions during the season.

Fig. J   *Erica cinerea*

Cultivars with white flowers
'Alba' Foliage – light green. Flower – smallish, produced in abundance. Plant is compact with relatively long spikes. *20 × 30*

'Alba Major' Foliage – deep green. Flower – only sparsely produced on the tips of the stems. Compact, neat and upright. An immaculate plant, almost worth growing for the foliage alone. 25 × 30

†'**Alba Minor**' (55) Foliage – light apple-green. Flower – in clusters, often so massed as to obscure the foliage. Small, extremely compact. 20 × 25

Fig. K   A raceme, often called a 'spike' (*Erica cinerea*)

'**Domino**' Foliage – dark green. Flower – white corolla, dark chocolate anthers. Habit is rather loose, with long flowering sprays. Apart from being a good garden plant this is interesting botanically, for it is the corolla alone which exhibits the normal characteristics associated with an albino, the rest of the plant, calyx, foliage, etc. being more like that of a coloured form. 25 × 35

[148]

'**Duncan Fraser**' Foliage – deep green. Flower – white, with merest pink blush, in strong spikes. Plant, vigorous and spreading. This much-admired recent introduction was found by Mr G. D. Waterer in Surrey and introduced by Knap Hill Nursery, Woking. 25 × 35

'**Hookstone White**' Foliage – pale green, darker on maturity. Flower – bells are pure white and more pointed in shape than usual. Although individually small they are produced in quantity on a long raceme. Tall. 30 × 35

'**Honeymoon**' (61) Foliage – pale green. Flowers – white, in small clusters. We read of these being 'washed with lavender on some soils' – a feature we have not ourselves observed. Found by Mr R. D. Trotter in 1927 this tiny grower has much reduced stems which arch from the centre of the plant and curl downwards to hug the ground. 10 × 15

'**Snow Cream**' Foliage – cream, yellow or green on different shoots. Older foliage flecked white. Unfortunately the foliage effect is not constant, and being unstable, is liable to revert to deep green. Flower – white, quite free.

Compact, fluffy appearance in its best form, but taller and more vigorous after reversion.

Lilac and bi-colour – mostly pale colours

'Apple Blossom' Foliage – light green. Flower – white on opening becoming palest pink. This name is often mistakenly given to 'Pallida'. *25 × 30*

'Cevennes' Foliage – light green. Flower – soft lavender with a hint of pink. Upright and compact. Introduced in the early 1930s from a plant brought back from France. *23 × 25*

†**'Eden Valley'** (57) Foliage – light green. Flower – bi-colour, each bell lilac with white base. Very free. Plant is low, arching – good spreader. *15 × 25*

'George Osmond' (66) Foliage – green, slightly glaucous. Flower – palest lavender, freely borne. Upright, delicate appearance. The pale-coloured corolla contrasts effectively with the dark foliage. Found by Mr George Osmond in Dorset many years ago, and still widely grown. *25 × 35*

'Hookstone Lavender' Foliage – pale green. Flower – light lavender bells in very long sprays. Distinct. Plant is vigorous and upright. *25 × 38*

'Lavender Lady' Foliage – pale green. Flower – pale lavender. Habit is loose, more spreading than upright. Found by Mr and Mrs Letts in Cornwall. *15 × 25*

'Lilacina' Foliage – light green. Flower – lilac pink, large bells. Semi-prostrate as a young plant becoming bushy with age. *20 × 35*

'Lilac Time' Similar to 'Lilacina' except that the growth is upright, dense. *20 × 25*

'Miss Waters' Foliage – dark green. Flower – white bells with distinct purple tip, later in the season becomes generally purple. Vigorous, bushy. This can be most attractive when producing its bi-colour effect, unfortunately for some reason best known to itself it will sometimes skip a season and simply have flowers of a dull purple. *30 × 40*

'Newick Lilac' (64) Foliage – bright green. Flower – clear lilac in long sprays. Plant is vigorous, upright. Bells are a delightful shade and the plant is of value for forming a contrast to the deeper colours. *25 × 30*

'Pallas' (88) Foliage – pale

green. Flower – pale-pinkish lavender. A strong grower with many stems of flowers in a good clear colour. This was formerly listed in Holland as 'Pallida' but has received a new name to distinguish it from the real 'Pallida' as the two are different. *30 × 40*

'Pallida' (91) Foliage – mid-green. Flower – very pale lilac with a trace of purple carried in long racemes. Growth is vigorous, bushy. More plants of this cultivar are sold as 'Apple Blossom' than under its true name. *30 × 38*

'Pink Foam' Foliage – dark green. Flower – pale pink, almost white, tinged with rose at the base. Will become bleached in strong sunlight; nevertheless a good contrast plant. Open, loose grower. *25 × 30*

Pink and red shades – mostly bright colours

'Atrorubens' Foliage – dark green. Flower – glowing red pink bells in long spikes. Compact. A superb introduction. *20 × 25*

†**'Atrosanguinea Smith's Variety'** (54 and 100) Foliage – dark green. Flower – bright red. The flowering shoots arch and when the first flush of bells begins to fade new stems appear with yet another crop. Low, open habit. *15 × 25*

†**'C. D. Eason'** (60, 79, 88 and 121) Foliage – deep green. Flower – brilliant deep pink in masses. Free growing, neat. One of the most popular of the brighter colour bell heathers, and justly so. *25 × 30*

'C. G. Best' Foliage – mid-green. Flower – clear light salmon in long sprays. Upright, floriferous with delicate appearance. *25 × 38*

'Coccinea' Foliage – very dark green. Flower – deep ruby bells in small clusters, often obscuring the foliage. Dwarf, prostrate. Usually the first of this group to flower, this is an admirable plant for the rock garden, front of border, chinks in crazy paving, etc. *10 × 30*

'Glasnevin Red' (63) Foliage – dark green. Flower – deep ruby-red bells carried on sturdy spikes. This seedling from 'C. D. Eason' will undoubtedly become very popular when it is generally available due to the striking dark-red coloration of the flowers. *20 × 25*

'Janet' (59) Foliage – pale green. Flower – soft shell-pink becoming milky-white. This attractive cultivar was found by Miss Waterer on Trink Hill, near Penzance, Cornwall – the same area in which she found 'Eden Valley'. *20 × 30*

'Knap Hill Pink' (62) Foliage – dark green. Flower – bright rose. Compact, dense. A reliable plant that produces a good display. This is the Knap Hill Nursery's improvement on the very old 'Rosea' and has flowers that are both deeper and brighter in colour. *15 × 25*

'Pink Ice' Foliage – mid-green with silver reverse. Flower – deep clear pink on opening becoming paler – the colour of pink coconut ice. Neat, compact and generous flowering. Found as a seedling in the Letts' garden. *10 × 25*

'Startler' (71) Foliage – fresh mid-green. Flower – bright pink, freely borne. Compact. Although eventually making a large plant it can be used in a rock garden planting, for as well as retaining its neat appearance it will always produce a good display even from an early age. *25 × 38*

'Stephen Davis' Foliage – deep glossy green. Flower – bright red. Compact. For sheer brilliance of colour this can hardly be surpassed. *15 × 25*

Purple or maroon shades – mostly deep colours

'Atropurpurea' Foliage – dark green. Flower – bright purple. Upright, vigorous. Similar to the usual wild form in colour, this is a good selection. *30 × 40*

'Cindy' Foliage – very dark green. Flower – bright deep purple closely packed towards the end of the long stems. Vigorous, prostrate at first becoming taller. *15 × 38*

'Colligan Bridge' Foliage – dark glossy green. Flower – reddish-purple on very thick branches. Extremely vigorous. Developed from a wild plant originally found growing by the roadside in Ireland. *30 × 45*

'Foxhollow Mahogany' (72) Foliage – deep green. Flower – dark maroon red in thick clusters. Although invariably starting off as a prostrate grower, it will become bushy after a season or so. An unusual and distinct colour. *15 × 30*

'Heathfield' Foliage – dark green. Flower – deep reddish-purple bells on long branching stems. Vigorous, tall. Introduced to cultivation by Treseders Nurseries.

'Joyce Burfitt' Foliage –

dull grey-green. Flower – dusky maroon bells on reddish stems. Plant, upright and dainty. Another unusual shade, making this a most desirable plant. Found by Miss Burfitt near her home in Dorset. *25 × 30*

'Katinka' Foliage – deep green. Flower – bright shining purple. Compact, very floriferous. We were very much taken with this new introduction from Holland at the Heather Trials in the Harlow Car Gardens, Harrogate. *28 × 35*

'My Love' (110) Foliage – very dark green. Flower – violet-blue on short spikes. Bushy and compact. *20 × 30*

'Pentreath' Foliage – dark green. Flower – deep reddish-purple freely produced. Semi-prostrate, good spreader. *20 × 30*

†**'P. S. Patrick'** Foliage – deep glossy green. Flower – rich purple bells on upright spikes. A very reliable and free flowering cultivar named after the finder, co-author of a standard book on heathers. This will be displayed to perfection if planted *en masse* with, say, a group of *Calluna* 'Gold Haze'. *30 × 38*

'Purple Beauty' Foliage – dark green. Flower – purple. Semi-prostrate with many large individual flowers. Vigorous. *20 × 38*

'Rozanne Waterer' Foliage – dark green. Flower – maroon-purple. Very prostrate. A lovely plant for a sunny sloping bank. Introduced by Knap Hill Nurseries. *15 × 40*

'Tilford' Foliage – deep green. Flower – bright purple in strong spikes. Compact, bushy. *30 × 40*

'Velvet Night' Foliage – a dark and glossy green. Flower – dark maroon-purple, this is one of the darkest colours to be found among all the heaths. Neat bushy habit. This very distinct plant was found in 1957 by Mr F. J. Stevens of the Maxwell and Beale Nursery, Dorset *23 × 25*

'Violetta' Foliage – deep green. Flower – violet bells in good spikes. This pretty plant was first grown by Mr W. Haalboom of Driebergen and is of a particularly clear colour. We came across it planted in the Van Gimborn Arboretum, near Doorn, Holland, where there are extensive plantings of heathers. *30 × 40*

'Vivienne Patricia' Foliage – deep green. Flower – blue-mauve in abundance. Compact. A free-flowering plant of an unusual colour found by Mr and Mrs Letts while holidaying in Cornwall, and named after Mrs Letts. *20 × 30*

The Guernsey Bell heathers
'Guernsey Lime' (56), **'Guernsey Pink', 'Guernsey Plum'** (121), **'Guernsey Purple'.**

These are a group of intriguing little heathers discovered by Mr David McClintock and Mr Ken Beckett on the coasts of Guernsey and Brecou, Channel Islands. Apart from the small size of the individual bells the most unusual feature is their prostrate, almost huddled form. The stems, instead of growing upright, arch over displaying clusters of bright flowers at the end of each one. With the exception of *E.c.* 'Guernsey Lime' the foliage is dark green, and the second name of each refers to the flower colour. Lime-green foliage turning orange-yellow in the winter separates 'Guernsey Lime' from the others. Its flowers are purple and make a pleasing contrast with the foliage colour. All have smaller individual bells than most forms of *E. cinerea* but are produced with abandon. The group as a whole should prove to be of value where large quick-growing plants are not needed – a position such as the rock garden.

Coloured foliage and coloured flowers
'Ann Berry' Foliage – lime green in summer becoming bright yellow gold in winter. Flower – deep purple. Loose, upright. Spotted by Mr Berry, a retired policeman, when walking across the common near his home at Chobham and introduced by Underwoods Nursery. *20 × 35*

'Apricot Charm' (38) Foliage – light yellow in summer. Winter colour is an unusual shade of apricot orange. Flower – purple, so sparse to date that they may be said to be virtually non-existent. However, well worth growing for the foliage effect alone. Very compact, delicate in appearance. *15 × 20*

'Constance' (73) Foliage – light golden with reddish tints often assuming a bright red coloration in Winter. Flower – deep purple bells in short terminal clusters. Upright, feathery. A single-coloured shoot which sported on 'P. S. Patrick' was encouraged to root. A stock of plants was built up and then named in honour of Mrs C. I. MacLeod as recognition for the work she has done as secretary of the Heather Society, almost since its inception. *25 × 30*

'Golden Drop' (81) Foliage – burnished gold turning fiery red in winter. Flower – mauve pink, seldom. Dense mat, prostrate. Does best where the soil is sharply drained and positioned in the full sun. *15 × 25*

'Golden Hue' Foliage – pale yellow, often red in winter. Flower – pale purple. Upright, rather thin growth. Unless trimmed liable to become straggly. *25 × 30*

'John Eason' (111) Foliage – shades of yellow, pale green and pink, turning rust in winter. Flower – soft salmon pink. Upright. *25 × 30*

'Rock Pool' Foliage – light golden-yellow assuming red and orange tints during colder weather. Flower – few, light purple. Prostrate, arching growth. This originated as a sport on a normal green plant and was given to Mr John Hall of Windlesham, who propagated it and named it. *15 × 25*

ERICA TETRALIX (the cross-leaved heath)

Our third familiar moorland plant with *E. cinerea* and *Calluna*. In nature it favours the wetter spots, but in the garden will grow well in normal soils. In common with other summer-flowering heaths, *E. tetralix* demands a lime-free soil if it is to thrive. Although fairly quick growing, they generally do not make very large plants and are seldom found to be higher than 30 cm. The flowers, which are described as ovoid, urceolate or oval pitcher-shaped, are produced on the current season's growth and are arranged in a cluster at the ends of the branched upright stems. In most cases the foliage is an added attraction, being silvery grey, indeed the cultivar known as 'Alba Mollis' is well worth growing

Fig. L   *Erica tetralix*

for its silver grey foliage alone. Starting to bloom in early summer, the flowering season is so long that it will be well into the autumn before it is finished.

Fig. M   An umbel-like cluster (*Erica tetralix*)

White and bi-colour flowers
Albino forms are found occasionally in the wild. Several have been collected and distributed under the cultivar name of 'Alba'. A typical plant has pure white flowers and foliage of a pleasing shade of light green.

†**'Alba Mollis'** (49) Foliage – frosted light silver becoming greener with age. Flower – pure white. Tight, compact and rather upright. This is a striking plant quite indispensable in the heather garden. *20 × 30*

'Alba Praecox' An earlier flowering white form of the cross-leaved heath. *20 × 30*

'Melbury White' Foliage – silver-grey. Flowers – white on many branched stems. Treseders of Truro introduced this cultivar which has large bells, freely produced and commencing early in the season. *15 × 20*

'Ruby's Variety' Foliage – light grey. Flower – off-white with pale pink flush. The open end of the corolla is ringed with bright purple. Often the bells will be simply pale pink. Loose, open straggly habit remedied by light trimming early each spring. *15 × 25*

'Silver Bells' Foliage – green. Flower – palest mauve with a silvery hue. Dwarf, slow growing. *20 × 30*

Pink flowers
'Darleyensis' Foliage – dull grey-green. Flower – soft salmon-pink bells with red markings at the mouth of the corolla. Stems criss-cross and curl around to form a mat-like springy plant. *15 × 30*

'Foxhome' Foliage – light grey-green. Flower – rose-pink. Distinguished by its neat manner of growth. Found by the late Fred Chapple near Whaley Bridge. 20 × 30

†'Hookstone Pink' Foliage – light silver. Flower – clear light rose with deeper tip. Upright, growth is loose at first becoming more dense with age. A beautiful colour, unlike any other heather. 30 × 25

'Jean Liddle' (U.S., of possible Dutch origin) Foliage – grey-green. Flower – bright mauve-pink. Open and branching, unusually tall for a plant in this group. 30 × 20

'L. E. Underwood' (51) Foliage – grey. Flower – light salmon-pink from apricot buds. A smaller growing plant named after Mr Les Underwood who together with his late brother, G. E. Underwood, started the Hookstone Green Nursery. Between them they have introduced a number of the most outstanding cultivars of *E. tetralix*. 15 × 25

'Mary Grace' Foliage – grey-green. Flower – bright pink with milky white base. Typically but not always the corolla is split into several segments. Sometimes this effect can look pleasant but can appear to be rather ragged. Low and spreading. 15 × 25

'Pink Star' Foliage – light silver-grey. Flower – bright lilac rose, starlike, with the bells clustered at the tips of the stems, facing upwards and outwards instead of down as with all the other cultivars. Loose floppy habit when young. 15 × 25

Another newcomer, similar but taller, is 'Helma' (50). Flower colour a little paler.

Darker colours

†'Con Underwood' Foliage – grey-green. Flower – crimson purple bells. Upright, neat habit. This is a superb free flowering form that can be recommended for a long-lasting display. 25 × 30

'Daphne Underwood' Similar to foregoing with somewhat larger individual bells and a lower more spreading growth. 15 × 25

'Ken Underwood' Foliage – dark grey. Flower – dusky maroon-purple, some white showing on the underside of the bells. Rather slow at first. Eventually forms an upright open twiggy bush. 25 × 30

ERICA MACKAIANA
(Mackay's heath)

Rather like a small version of *E. tetralix* – the cross-leaved heath, so it is not difficult to see why this has sometimes been included with that species. It is a native to the British Isles, occurring as a rare plant in north-west Ireland, and is also found in north-west Spain. Like the cross-leaved heath it favours the wetter spots in the wild, but is quite happy with normal soil as a garden plant, providing it is lime free. All are low growing. It has had a part in producing some good hybrids.

Fig. N *Erica mackaiana*: single (*left*), 'Plena' (*right*)

'William M'Alla' (44) Foliage – deep green. Flower – deep rose in terminal clusters. In suitable soil will make a dense spreading plant. *20 × 25*

'Lawsoniana' Foliage – deep green. Flower – pale rose lilac. A pleasing little plant that is not so often seen nowadays. *15 × 25*

'Plena' (41) Foliage – deep green often assuming purple shades in winter. Flower – fully double, the deep rose bells are frilled at the tips and have a white centre. More prostrate growing than others of this species, it is best on a rock garden as the flowers that hang down in clusters are not too easily seen when planted on the level. *12 × 25*

'Dr Ronald Gray' (48) Foliage – light green. Flower – pure white in clusters. An interesting new development from a plant of 'Lawsoniana' found by and named after the late Dr Ronald Gray of Hindhead, Surrey. *15 × 25*

ERICA TERMINALIS (E. STRICTA) (The Corsican heath)

Although originating in the Mediterranean area, this plant will prove perfectly hardy in a normal winter here, although the upright stems can suffer rather from heavy snow. Growing to over 2 metres in height it is often listed among the tree heaths and sold as a specimen for the heather borders, etc. The flowers are produced in terminal clusters. The individual bells are clear rose and make a pleasing contrast with

Fig. O   *Erica terminalis*

the apple-green foliage. Completely tolerant of lime, this will also do well in a moderately heavy soil flowering from mid-summer until late autumn. Until recently the type only was grown, but we now have a cultivar. *60 × 25*

'Thelma Woolner' Foliage – dark green. Flower –

deep rose becoming paler. Compact, dwarfer and more floriferous than the type.

Mr Woolner tells us how he came to find this distinct break, 'When my wife and I were in Sardinia in 1967, we found at a height of over 3000 feet, a small colony of *E. terminalis*, some plants of which had flowers of a deeper colour than the type.' Cuttings were collected from the best plant and brought back and rooted. It has since proved to be a worthwhile introduction, bearing rather deeper colour flowers than the previous form grown. *45 × 40*

SUMMER-FLOWERING HYBRIDS

Where two species of some *Ericas* grow near by, there is a remote chance that they will successfully cross-pollinate, when the resulting seedlings will be hybrids and more or less intermediate between the parents. Unless collected by some keen-eyed gardener they are likely to die out and the plant be lost forever as some are more or less sterile. Sometimes they will back cross to one of their parents. This happens rarely between the hybrid of *E. ciliaris* and *E.*

tetralix (*Erica* x *watsonii*) to form what is known as a hybrid swarm. Some of the plants lean more towards one parent than the other. From the garden point of view, the first crosses are better as they are more distinct.

Not all the native species cross to form hybrids. None are known with *E. cinerea* as one of the parents, neither has *Calluna* been definitely proved to do this. Cultivation is similar to that of the parent species and none of the summer-flowering hybrids will tolerate lime in any form.

ERICA x PRAEGERI (E. MACKAIANA x E. TETRALIX)

Foliage – grey green. Flower – small light rose-pink in clusters flowering over a long period. Upright, yet compact grower. This is the original introduction grown for many years. *25 × 30*

The undermentioned clones have recently been introduced by Mr David McClintock who has made several trips to those parts of Ireland where the parent species grow wild. A remarkable coincidence regarding these finds is that he selected 'Irish Lemon' and 'Irish Orange' for the size and colour of their flowers and did not discover the added bonus of the brilliant new growth until they were growing on in his own garden.

Fig. P   *Erica* x *praegeri*

'Irish Lemon' (**39 and 40**) Foliage – light clear lemon starting in spring and carrying on for several weeks. Older foliage deep green making a pleasing contrast. Flower – light purple in clusters as in *E. tetralix* but the colour is brighter and bells larger. Neat compact habit. *20 × 25*

'Irish Orange' Another new cultivar with bright orange new growth in the spring, this too lasting for several weeks. Flowers – similar in colour to the foregoing but opening rather later.

Erica 'Stuartii' (108)

This plant is a puzzle, for no one seems to be able to say what are the parents or if it is indeed a hybrid. A single clump discovered growing in Ireland at the end of the last century, it rather resembles a close compact-growing *E. tetralix* when young, although the foliage is a different colour and flowers not of the same shape. This is a plant that deserves a place in a collection of heathers for it is both showy and has a long flowering period. Foliage – dark green. Flower – tubular rose-pink. The end of the bell is pinched and deep red. *25 × 30*

ERICA x *WATSONII* (*E. CILIARIS* x *E. TETRALIX*)

Most of the crosses have come from the 'Great Heath', that wonderful stretch of heather and gorse that extends from near Wareham out towards Studland in the Isle of Purbeck. With the Dorset Lakes on one side and the rolling Purbeck Hills as a background this is one of the best places in Britain to see *E. ciliaris* growing in a reasonable quantity. There is plenty of *E. tetralix* here too – hence the hybrids.

That great heather enthusiast and author, D. F. Maxwell, together with his staff, were responsible for collecting and introducing all of the cultivars we know today. 'H. Maxwell' was named after his father; 'Dawn' and 'Gwen' were named after two nieces of his then partner, H. E. Beale. All this group need acid conditions, the plants thriving in a rich humus soil. They have the foliage and the flowers of the Dorset heath, the stature and long flowering time of the cross-leaved heath.

A word of warning here to the precise gardener who wishes his plants to be correctly named. These cultivars are thoroughly mixed up in nurseries. One often gets 'H. Maxwell' instead of 'Dawn' and vice versa. These are all rather alike in the young stage when it would need a specialist to tell them apart. There is no mistaking 'Gwen' however, for the colour is unlike any other. 'F. White', too, is different. All flower from early summer until early autumn.

Fig. Q   *Erica* x *watsonii*

†**'Dawn'** (122) Foliage – clear yellow and tangerine tips to the new growth, becoming deep green. Flower – deep rose-pink, large rounded bells. Compact bushy habit. *15 × 30*

'F. White' Foliage – grey-green. Flower – rather narrow, white with deep pink tips becoming more generally flushed pale purple. The flowers themselves are held in short racemes rather like the Dorset heath. Rather more compact than the others. *15 × 30*

'Gwen' Foliage – light grey-green with early spring growth of pale lemon, tipped bright red. Flower – pale rose lavender almost globose in shape. Too pale a colour to be grown separately, but useful to introduce a contrast between brighter-coloured varieties. Dwarf spreading habit. *15* × *30*

'H. Maxwell' Foliage – dark-green; eglandular young growth is of a bronze yellow, tipped red. Flower – deep pink. Upright, brittle growth. *30* × *25*

ERICA x *WILLIAMSII* (*E. VAGANS* x *E. TETRALIX*)

The two named clones both originated in Cornwall on the Lizard Peninsula where the two parents are growing adjacently. They are both excellent garden plants, worth having for their pretty foliage as well as their floriferous nature and where quick ground cover is needed. The soil must be lime free but it does not matter if it is on the heavy side for they will thrive in such conditions.

The display could be six or more months long from these plants, starting in spring with the brightly coloured young foliage, followed by masses of flowers in early summer and continuing through to the autumn. The flowers are borne in a short cluster rather resembling that of the Cornish heath except that in this case it does not taper to a point but is more umbellate.

Foliage too is similar but smaller, and less rigid and glandular hairy, the stems radiating outwards from the plant instead of growing in an upright fashion.

Fig. R   *Erica* x *williamsii*

'Gwavas' Foliage – pale yellow in spring becoming lime green contrasting with the deep green of the mature foliage. Flower – pale rose in small clusters. Loose habit and lesser height distinguish it from the more commonly grown 'P. D. Williams'. *15* × *30*

†**'P. D. Williams'** (58) Foliage – creamy yellow at first, becoming deep yellow, pale green and finally shiny green with bronze tints in cold weather. Flowers are a little darker than the foregoing.

(Formerly known as 'Williamsiana' and still sometimes listed as such.) 20 × 40

DABOECIA CANTABRICA
(St Dabeoc's heath)
Quite unlike any of the other heathers in general appearance, these plants from southwest Ireland and northern Spain are valuable additions to any heather garden on lime-free soil. The usual wild colour is a pale rose, but a wide range of colours is available for the planter to choose from. The flowers range from pure white to pink and deep purple. Both the flowers and foliage differ from the rest of the heaths inasmuch as the individual corolla is large and is carried in a long leafless spike well above the wide shiny leaves. The under-surface of the leaf is covered in fine white hair which imparts a silvery appearance when the foliage is lifted.

Flowering from early summer, or late spring in some instances, continuing right through to early autumn and the first of the frosts, each bell is so large that the bumble bees in search of honey cannot reach down with their tongues as do the honey bees, but have

the ingenuity to cut a small hole at the side near the base in order to take a short cut!

When the flower is fertilized the corolla drops off, while still coloured, instead of remaining on the plant until brown as do the *Ericas*. Spent flower stems can be removed immediately they are finished, or left for seed until the following spring.

This species is not among the hardiest, sometimes getting cut back in a hard winter, but more often than not breaking from the base again.

Fig. S   *Daboecia cantabrica*

White and bi-coloured flowering cultivars
alba Foliage – light glossy green. Flower – large pure

white bells. A vigorous grower that will at times produce many white seedlings of varying worth, mostly in the garden and rarely in the wild. Some of these are shy of flowering and ought to be discarded. Two recent selections of notable worth which can be regarded as improvements of the original are 'David Moss', a compact grower, and 'Snowdrift'. *38 × 45*

'Alba Globosa' is similar to *alba* except the individual bells are more rounded and larger, although probably not so freely produced. *38 × 45*

'Bicolor' Foliage – deep green. Flower – white, pale pink, purple and striped. An unusual break that gives a worthwhile display from the novelty of having separate colours on the same plant, and even on the same bell. *38 × 40*

'Cinderella' Foliage – greyish, dark green. Flowers – white, each bell having a slight blush of rose-pink at the base. A sport from *Daboecia cantabrica* 'Polifolia', the white flowers are a marked contrast to the dark foliage. *30 × 35*

'Donard Pink' Foliage – dark-green leaves, margin purple. Flower – unusual pale pink, some stems produce white bells. Upright. Introduced by the Slieve Donard Nursery, Northern Ireland. *38 × 40*

Pink and purple shades

'Atropurpurea' Foliage – dark bronze green. Flower – rich warm purple in strong spikes. A favourite colour and one that can be relied upon to make a good show each summer. Bushy, strong grower. *40 × 45*

'Globosa' Foliage – deep green. Flower – rose-purple, very large. This is the most vigorous of the Daboecias. It has correspondingly larger bells that are more rounded. *40 × 45*

'Hookstone Purple' Foliage – dark green. Flower – rounded, dull purple. Vigorous habit, raised and introduced by the late George Underwood, West End, Woking. *35 × 40*

†**'Polifolia'** Foliage – light greyish green, veins red. Flower – pale lilac rose. A good cultivar for a contrast in colour, that although similar in colour to the native plant, both the growth and flowers are better. *30 × 40*

'Porters Variety' Foliage – minute leaves of dark green. Flower – dark crimson, narrow tubular. A small upright grower. *15 × 20*

'Praegerae' Foliage – dark green with purplish sheen, silvery undersides. Flower – clear salmon pink. Spreading. In our opinion one of the finest heathers ever introduced. *25 × 38*

Daboecia hybrids

In recent years some very good smaller plants have arrived on the 'heather scene'. These have perhaps come about as the result of the crossing of two species, the usually tender *D. azorica* and the hardier *D. cantabrica*. Longer flowering and with brighter colours than either of their parents they are a valuable addition to the existing range. We have grown them for a number of years and early fears that they would not prove hardy appear to be unfounded.

'Bearsden' Foliage – large, dark glossy green. Flower – deep purple-red. Dwarf compact habit. Raised and introduced by Miss Logan Home, Edrom Nurseries, Scotland, from seed of *D. azorica*. A most attractive garden-worthy plant. *25 × 30*

'Cora' Foliage – dark green, small. Flowers – pale pink in short spikes, large for the general proportions of the plant. Believed to be a seedling from *D.* 'William Buchanan'. *15 × 15*

†**'William Buchanan'** (47) (**Seedling No. 1**) Foliage – dark shiny green. Flower – rose-purple in short spikes. This is the largest of three seedlings which originally appeared in the garden of the late William Buchanan at Bearsden. They were given to Mr Jack Drake, the alpine grower, for propagation and for introduction to cultivation. This clone is vigorous and flowers well over an exceptionally long period. *25 × 30*

'Seedling No. 3' (84) Foliage – dark glossy green. Flower – small, dark red bells. A charming little plant that is a half-size version of the other seedling. The small flowers are a clear dark red without the purple usually seen in others with similar colouring. In appearance rather similar to *D. azorica*, but hardier. *15 × 30*

ERICA VAGANS (Cornish heath)

This species grows in the Lizard area of Cornwall, Brittany, south-west France, northern

Spain and in one small patch in Ireland. The wild plant has mostly pale pinkish purple flowers – not an exciting colour! However, there are some very beautiful coloured forms that have been introduced into our gardens as well as some of our best white-flowered summer heathers. These are plants that thrive in a heavier soil

Fig. T *Erica vagans*

than many of the other heaths and will also tolerate a moderately alkaline soil, but do still add plenty of peat in such situations. Individual bells are tiny but are arranged in closely packed flower spikes either long and tapering as in 'Cream' or shorter and more cylindrical as 'Kevernensis Alba'. The lower bells often fade to russet while the topmost are still opening. This does not detract

from the beauty of the plant, and even when the entire inflorescence is over these russet bells are retained as an added feature throughout the winter. They may be trimmed lightly to shape in the spring removing all the old flowers. Their habit of growth is invariably neat and they are excellent for filling in large areas in the heather garden where quick ground cover is required, coupled with a long lasting display of bright colour during summer and autumn.

Cultivars with white flowers
'Alba' Foliage – vivid green. Flower – white, with reddish-brown anthers. Free flowering, vigorous. *30 × 40*
  'Cream' (119) Foliage – mid-green. Flower – white, becoming creamy white, the pinkish tinge probably due to the colour of the anthers showing through the side of the corolla. Flower spikes rather loose but of a good size. Tall, vigorous. *45 × 50*
 'Kevernensis Alba' Foliage – deep green. Flower – white with yellowish anthers freely produced on short spikes. Compact. *25 × 40*
 †**'Lyonesse'** (113) Foliage – deep fresh green. Flower –

[165]

white with gold anthers. Very floriferous and long lasting. Tall, upright and fairly quick growing. The flowers must be a good source of honey judging by the amount of bees they attract. *35 × 45*

'White Rocket' Foliage – dull green. Flower – white in extremely long narrow tapering spikes. Tall, vigorous. Introduced by Treseders Nursery, Truro. *38 × 45*

Pink and pale shades
'Geo. Underwood' Foliage – light green. Flower – creamy pink in long tapering spikes. Compact. *30 × 45*

'Holden Pink' Foliage – dull green. Flower – white, flushed pink. Bushy, upright. *30 × 40*

'Lilacina' Foliage – dull green. Flower – palest rose lilac in profusion. Compact, bushy. 'Pallida' is virtually identical. *30 × 45*

'Mrs Donaldson' Foliage – mid-green. Flower – pale peach, early flowering and most attractive when just opening. Compact, bushy. *30 × 45*

†**'St Keverne'** Foliage – fresh vivid green. Flower – bright rose in abundance. Compact, bushy. Many pink cultivars have been raised, named

and introduced, but few come anywhere near this in quality of flowers and general appearance. *25 × 30*

'Summertime' Foliage – mid-green. Flower – soft milky white, a pretty delicate shade which contrasts well with the deeper shades. Compact. Introduced by the Slieve Donard Nursery, Northern Ireland. *25 × 30*

Red and purple shades
'Diana Hornibrook' (**96 and 134**) Foliage – fresh green. Flower – cerise red, similar to that of 'Mrs D. F. Maxwell' but flowering begins a few weeks earlier. Compact. *25 × 30*

'Fiddlestone' Foliage – fresh green. Flower – cerise/ dark red. Regarded by many as an improvement on 'Mrs D. F. Maxwell' bearing similar coloured flowers. From our own experience we would suggest both are very good but too similar for garden purposes. *25 × 30*

†**'Mrs D. F. Maxwell'** (**117, 120 and 136**) Foliage – deep glossy green. Flower – cerise/ dark red. Neat bushy growth with long spikes. This outstanding plant was found by Mr and Mrs D. F. Maxwell

when honeymooning in Cornwall. This was a great improvement on any other heather grown previously and is still possibly the most popular summer-flowering variety. *25 × 35*

'Pyrenees Pink' (115) Foliage – fresh green. Flower – light red in short spikes. As the lower bells on the flower spikes fade to pale russet the plant assumes a bi-colour effect. **25 × 30**

'Rubra' (124) Foliage – dark green. Flower – deep mulberry pink in long spikes. One of the older introductions with an unusual colour flower. Vigorous, spreading. *30 × 40*

Coloured foliage

'Valerie Proudley' (10 and 141) Foliage – of a particularly bright nature – especially so in winter. New growth light gold, older foliage lime green. Flower – white but sparse. Originally occurred in 1965 as a single aberrant shoot on a normal green plant. Instead of trying to root this from a cutting we decided to defoliate the entire plant with the exception of the one golden branch. Later, after it had grown considerably, the plant was lifted and replanted, this time with the single-coloured shoot only showing above the surface. The following season the plant was lifted again and discarded after removing the now well-rooted golden portion. Cuttings were then taken from which the entire stock has been raised. Growth is fairly slow, eventually making a small dense bush. *15 × 25*

ERICA CILIARIS (Dorset heath)
When in flower this must surely be one of our most beautiful native plants, although in the wild they usually have a rather straggly growth. More common on the Continent than Britain where it is found in France, Spain and Portugal. There is plenty on the 'Great Heath' in the county which name it bears. It is less frequent in Cornwall, and very rare in Devon and Co. Galway.

We have mentioned the straggly nature of this species, but this is readily overcome in the garden plants by careful trimming in early spring from the first season of planting. This is another species that does not survive in limy soil – so plenty of peat for this one.

The flowers, larger than in all the other hardy species of

Erica, are urn-shaped and are carried in racemes at the ends of the stems.

The foliage is soft to the touch and usually rather sticky. The whole plant is brittle and will damage easily (this is intended as a warning to owners of dogs and small children).

Fig. U   *Erica ciliaris*

E. ciliaris is the least hardy of our native heaths and is not suitable for very cold places where stem splitting or worse can occur. Flowering is from mid-summer until late autumn. (Together with *E. tetralix* this has produced some outstanding hybrids.)

White and bi-colour

'David McClintock' (52) Foliage – light grey. Flower – white with deep pink tips. Sometimes the whole corolla becomes pale pink especially late in the season. Collected by Mr David McClintock, who found the original plant near Carnac in Brittany mixed inextricably (as he described it) with a gorse bush. This was given to us to propagate. A good stock was soon built up and the resulting plants were exhibited at one of the R.H.S. shows in 1968 and there named after the finder. *25 × 38*

'Stapehill' Foliage – pale green. Flower – pinkish with white base, deep pink tip. Although not as bi-coloured as the previous cultivar, it is none the less an attractive plant which was introduced by the late 'Charlie' Marchant of Keepers Hill Nursery, near Wimborne, Dorset. *25 × 38*

'Stoborough' Foliage – light fresh green. Flower – pure white. This is by far the tallest of the group reaching as high as 60 cm at times. There are conflicting claims as to who discovered the original of this outstanding plant. *35 × 40*

'White Wings' Foliage –

deep green. Flower – pure white. Mrs Vivienne Letts was the finder of this pretty sport. Working in her garden one day she noticed a single branch on the cultivar 'Mrs C. H. Gill' was producing white flowers instead of the usual reddish-purple. Propagated, it has remained white. *30 × 40*

Pink and purple shades
'Corfe Castle' (53) Foliage – mid-green, sometimes turns purplish in winter. Flower – clear salmon. An outstanding recent introduction by Mr George Osmond of Wickwar, who found it when on a visit to the Corfe Castle area. He told us he had just stopped the car to have a look at the Dorset Heaths in flower, and there it was! Yet we have tramped for miles over the same area and have never found anything out of the ordinary – an enjoyable pastime none the less! *25 × 35*

'Globosa' (133) (Holland– 'Norden') Foliage – grey-green. Flower – clear pink, more rounded than normal. An old cultivar which could be regarded as a selected form of the native plant. Virtually the same as the cultivar 'Rotundiflora' sometimes listed. *30 × 35*

'Maweana' Foliage – grey. Flower – dark purple pink. Almost prostrate when young but soon becoming more bushy as it matures. This is a superb plant when grown well. Originating in Portugal and possibly the least hardy of this group. *20 × 30*

'Mrs C. H. Gill' Foliage – dark green. Flower – reddish-purple. Flowers are rather on the small side but are carried in profusion. *25 × 38*

'Wych' Foliage – pale green. Flower – palest flesh pink, a quantity of pinched bells. Upright. *30 × 35*

Coloured foliage
'Aurea' Foliage – light golden-yellow with orange-yellow young growths. Flower – purple but sparse. This plant has to be sited carefully to succeed, out of the wind to prevent scorch damage to the foliage, yet in the full sun to get the true colour. Definitely worth persevering with. *25 × 35*

CALLUNA VULGARIS
This wild plant, adapted by nature to exist in some of the most bleak and inclement places, occurs in such conditions over most of Europe extending from the north of

Norway to the southern tip of Spain, and just reaches North Africa. This is the predominant late summer- and autumn-flowering plant of vast stretches of moorland and mountain, and is so familiar that we feel a detailed description is unnecessary.

Although the genus *Calluna* contains but a single species the variations that have occurred in the wild or in the garden are exceedingly numerous and range from low creeping plants mere centimetres high, up to others of one metre or more.

The puce coloration of the wild plant gives way to bright scarlet, deep purple, various shades of pink and of course white. Several have attractively filled double flowers with many layers of petals. These last in flower considerably longer than their single counterparts. Some of the finest coloured foliage forms also occur within these variations from clear yellow to the lovely sunset shades of soft orange, bronze and red.

Like the wild 'ling' the garden plants demand a lime-free soil rich in peat. They stand wind, and as natural plants of the cliff-tops they have what is known as a

'Maritime Inheritance' or an ability to flourish where salt-laden breezes blow!

The species is late summer and autumn flowering but some of the garden forms flower outside of this time, covering the period from early summer until late autumn. In the descriptive list that follows we have noted these as being early or late, where no time of flowering is given it may be taken these will be out during late summer, mid-autumn. Annual trimming of the old flower stems is probably more important with this species than any of the others, for if this is ignored the plants may eventually become leggy and also lack flowers.

Correctly trimmed they will form a nice compact plant with plenty of foliage and good flower spikes. The usual recommendation is to prune after the flowers fade, but we prefer to do ours during early spring just before the new growth begins.

Just how hard to cut back seems to cause the most worries; many would rather not prune than make a mistake, but too light a trimming is more common than too hard. Once one understands why it has to be done nothing could be simpler. Take a look at an unpruned plant of, say, *Calluna* 'Elsie Purnell' – we have chosen this as an example for it has probably one of the longest flowering sprays of all. Starting at the top of the shoot there is a nice plump green tip with the

Fig. V *Calluna vulgaris:* double flowers (*left*), single (*right*)

dead double flowers arranged down the stem. Below these old flowers we come to more green foliage. This is where we make the cut – just into the green foliage, removing all the old flower stem complete with green tip. Left to its own devices the plant will grow away from the green tip, the old flowers drop off leaving a bare stem, for new growth does not start from where the flowers were, only from above or below. Of course there will be many stems to cut and a pair of garden shears is about the best tool for the job. Unlike roses and other shrubs there is no need to prune to a bud or anything like that, but just back to the foliage.

White flowers – single
alba ('Lucky' White Heather) is the name given to the white forms of the wild plant although they can vary considerably and each 'find' when cultivated could in fact receive a separate cultivar name. Many of the white heathers are virtually indistinguishable from each other, but a selection is described here briefly. They are useful as cut flowers as well as for garden decoration.

'Alba Aurea' Foliage – dark green with golden tips to new growth. Low, early. *10 × 25*

'Alba Carlton' Foliage – dark green. Loose spreading growth. Flowers on both spikes and laterals. *35 × 45*

'Alba Jae' Foliage – light green, short sprays packed with flowers. *25 × 30*

'Alba Minor' (79) Tiny flowers on stems radiating out above the fresh green foliage. *20 × 25*

†**'Alba Rigida'** (60) Forms a tight low-growing plant with bright green foliage bearing short compact sprays of flowers. *15 × 25*

'August Beauty' Very long tapering flower spikes, the lower of which sometimes twists downwards. The foliage is light at first becoming darker with maturity. *45 × 50*

'Beoley Elegance' Thin upright stems with wide open flowers. Foliage, dark green. An excellent plant raised by Mr J. W. Sparkes and used by him in his cut heather business. Mid to late flowering. *30 × 45*

'Caerketton White' Forms a rounded rather twiggy plant with many sprays of flowers. Fresh green foliage. Early and long flowering. *25 × 25*

'Calf of Man' ('White Carpet') Rather like 'Alba Rigida' at first sight but this appears to be quicker growing with longish sprays of flowers on a prostrate-growing plant. *10 × 25*

'Crispa' (U.S.A.) An attractive plant of American origin. The green tips at the ends of the flowering spikes develop after flowering into a crinkly tuft. Light yellow green foliage, low growing although possibly taller in the States. *30 × 30*

'Cunneryensis' Long sprays on an open growing tall plant. Deep green foliage. Late flowering makes this a useful cultivar to have. *35 × 40*

'Drum-Ra' Another tall although rather stiffer grower, branches varying in height. Fresh green foliage. *40 × 30*

'Dumosa' Upright with compact growth. An old cultivar more popular in Holland than Britain. *25 × 35*

'Elegantissima' Foliage – bright green. Flowers – pure white in strong tapering spikes. Well grown it is magnificent and a favourite in Holland where this was raised and is often met with. *30 × 45*

'Elkstone' Tiny plant with bright green foliage and small sprays of flowers. Found and propagated by Mr John Ravenscroft, this is now one of the most popular for its early and continuous flowering. Neat low growth. *15 × 30*

†**'Hammondii'** Foliage – dark bright green. Flower – in long solid spikes. One of the oldest heathers in cultiva-

tion, yet still regarded as one of the best of the whites. *40 × 50*

'Hammondii   Aurea' Could almost go in the coloured foliage section for its golden new shoots which contrast rather well with the dark green of the older foliage. The display of flowers is rather short lived. *40 × 50*

'Hugh Nicholson' A colourful spring foliage plant named by Mr J. W. Sparkes after a popular Heather Society member. The new growth is cream and deepens to bright yellow, contrasting well with the older dark-green foliage. Generous sprays of flowers displayed over several weeks to follow. *30 × 25*

'Humpty Dumpty' (105) Foliage fresh mossy green. Habit of growth is uneven, and tufted. A low-growing variety suitable for the rock garden. This is not grown for its flowers (being rather sparse) as much as a novelty. *10 × 14*

'Hirsuta Albiflora' Soft hairy greyish green foliage. Much like 'Silver King' and 'White Gown' which are more likely to be met with. *30 × 40*

'Kirby White' A foliage plant of merit with golden tips to the young growth. Older foliage dark green. Most attractive when in flower. 'Ruby Slinger' appears to be identical. *30 × 35*

'Kit Hill' A dwarf grower flowering well on both main spikes and laterals. The sprays curve outwards from the centre of the plant. *20 × 30*

'Long White' (Holland). Open upright growth with exceptionally long flowering sprays which are most suitable for cutting. A late flowering introduction. *40 × 50*

'Mair's Variety' One of the most vigorous growers, producing long tapering spikes. Another tall-growing cultivar with pale foliage at first, becoming darker. *50 × 45*

'October White' Tall erect plant which flowers late in the season and another which is useful for the flower arranger. *40 × 45*

'Serlei' (116) Soft dark-green foliage with strong upright sprays of flowers appearing rather late in the season. An old and distinguished cultivar. Tall and late. *40 × 50*

'Shirley' Although often spoken of as the same plant as 'Serlei', our plants which came from Holland via a nurseryman friend, although similar, are a full month earlier and normally grow to but half the height. *25 × 40*

'Silver King' Soft green foliage covered with fine white hairs giving a silvery appearance. Better foliage than 'White Gown' which it resembles, but we do not consider it outstanding enough to be placed in the foliage section. *30 × 35*

'Silver Spire' Upright, well-flowered plant with bright green foliage at all times. The 'Silver' in the name refers to the flowers and not the foliage as in 'Silver Queen' and 'Silver Knight'. *30 × 35*

'Spring Cream' Foliage – bright cream new growth on deeper green of old foliage. Upright but compact. *25 × 25*

'Tenella' This has thin branches with delicate flowering stems that grow in a rather congested manner. *25 × 25*

'Torulosa' Thin tapering spikes with buds still opening as the lower flowers fade. A dainty long flowering plant. It is essential to prune hard to maintain vigour, or the dainty effect will become lost on a woody plant. Although flowering at the normal time it also continues until quite late in the season. *30 × 40*

'White Gown' Soft plumose sprays of greyish-green foliage bearing generous racemes of white flowers. Mid to late. Fairly tall. *30 × 40*

'White Mite' A plant in which everything has been reduced except the quantity of the tiny flower stems. Foliage is bright green. Very early; in fact we have exhibited this in full bloom at the Chelsea Flower Show in late spring. *15 × 25*

White flowers – double

'Alba Plena' Foliage – pale to dark green. Flower – fully double in long sprays. Habit is rather prostrate and spreading. A superb plant that originated in Germany as a sport on a single white cultivar and it often starts flowering in single before the double flowers commence. Mid to late. *25 × 30*

'Else Frye' Flowers double as 'Alba Plena', and from the garden point of view almost identical although of entirely different origin. A seedling in America. *25 × 30*

'Kinlochruel' (69) Foliage – deep green becoming purplish green in winter. Flower – fully double, open wide and borne on short stems. A promising plant discovered by the late Brig. Ernest Montgomery growing as a sport on 'County Wicklow' and named after his house in Argyll. *20 × 25*

'White Bouquet' Sometimes listed, was a reversion on 'Ruth Sparkes', itself a sport of 'Alba Plena'. The plant resembles 'Alba Plena' in every respect. *25 × 30*

White-flowered cultivars with coloured foliage
'Beoley Gold' (80 and 123) Foliage – bright golden yellow. Flower – single pure white in short sprays. This is a strong sturdy grower that needs to be kept growing by good cultivation resulting in plenty of fresh foliage. If allowed to become starved or too dry it flowers rather more which when faded and brown spoils the lovely foliage effect. *38 × 45*

'Carole Chapman' Foliage – golden, shaded lime green. Flower – single and few. Habit is tufted when young with stems of varying heights. *15 × 30*

†**'Gold Haze'** (62, 91, 104 and 124) Foliage – clear yellow-gold. Flower – single in long sprays much like 'Beoley Gold' in appearance but a more delicate looking plant on the whole. Tall. *38 × 45*

'Ruth Sparkes' Foliage – bright golden-yellow especially so in winter. Flower – double in long sprays. Compact and spreading. This plant sometimes reverts to green 'Alba Plena' or even further to green with single white flowers. In this case remove the reverting branches where possible. Midseason. *15 × 35*

'Serlei Aurea' Foliage – soft feathery pale yellow deepening to gold in winter. Flower – single and not as freely borne as 'Serlei' from which this was a sport. Mid to late flowering. *45 × 45*

NOTE: *All with coloured foliage should be planted in full sun for best effect. Try to view the plants from the 'sunny' side if possible.*

Pink, purple and red single flowers
†**'Alportii'** (74) Foliage – dark green. Flower – reddish-purple in strong spikes. An old cultivar but still popular and justly so. Growth is vigorous and will soon form a large upright growing plant. *40 × 45*

'Alportii Praecox' Virtually the same flower as the foregoing but about two weeks earlier and growth is shorter and more spreading. *35 × 40*

'Barnett Anley' (123) Foliage – dull green. Flower – bright rose-purple heavily clustered at the base of the stem as well as the main spike. Raised by Mrs Anley from a seedling in her Woking garden. Medium to tall. Mid to late flowering. *35 × 40*

'Bronze Beauty' (U.S.A.) (sometimes known as 'Black Beauty') Seedling raised by the late Mrs E. Deutsch of Long Island. Most attractive when in bud, they are of a reddish colour and they do not open, but remain on the plant as in the manner of 'Underwoodii'. *30 × 40*

'Bradford' (U.S.A.) Foliage – dark green in dense low arching sprays. Flower – deep bright purple. Vigorous and spreading. *35 × 45*

'Californian Midge' (U.S.A.) A tiny plant with pale purple flowers. Used mainly in trough gardens and in small pockets on the rockery. This is similar to 'Nana Compacta' but with a light green foliage turning darker in winter. Sent to the late Fred Chapple by a friend in the U.S.A. *15 × 20*

'Carmen' (Holland) Foliage – deep green. Flowers – bright reddish-purple in densely packed spikes. Raised by Mr C. Bouter in Holland, it is said to be a sport from cultivar 'Barnett Anley' easily distinguished by the different colour of the flowers. *30 × 38*

'Coccinea' Foliage – light grey. Flower – dark crimson in short sprays. Forms a low rather twiggy shrub. *23 × 30*

'C. W. Nix' Foliage – dark green. Flower – reddish-purple, a shade lighter than 'Alportii'. Habit is graceful with long flowering stems that curve outwards. *40 × 35*

†**'Dainty Bess'** (U.S.A.) Foliage – soft grey on closely packed shoots. Flower – few, lavender in tiny spikes. This American introduction is like 'Sister Anne' but rather flatter in growth and a little more open. *10 × 25*

'Darkness' (**125 and 130**) Foliage – soft bright green. Flower – bright crimson with a hint of purple. Compact dense grower with a generous amount of flower.

Mr M. C. Pratt formerly of Wirral, Cheshire, who raised it, told us that he had the plant for a number of years before realizing its worth. We now regard it as the finest of those with similar colouring, both for the neat compact growth and the prolific amount of bloom. *30 × 38*

'Darleyensis' Foliage – bronze green, becoming darker in winter. Flower – salmon pink becoming reddish. The tip of the flowering spike often curls around and develops in an unusual way. The plant eventually forms a large growing hummock which we consider to be attractive during the late summer.

Almost certainly incorrectly named in Britain. It is known as 'Brachysepala Densa' both in Holland and in the U.S.A. *23 × 35*

'David Eason' (114) Foliage – light green, rather spreading growth. Flower – red-purple egg-shaped buds do not open, but fade to creamy white and are retained throughout the winter. Found in Dorset by Mr Eason, an Australian who was working at Maxwell and Beale's Nursery at the time. *23 × 38*

'Durfordii' Foliage – dark green becoming purplish-green during cold weather. Flower – rose-purple, very late. Useful as it flowers at a time when colour in the heather garden is scarce. *30 × 40*

'E. F. Brown' Foliage – light green, very open. Flower – pale lilac in good spikes. This useful introduction from America found in Germany is similar to the old 'Pallida' which is seldom seen these days. *35 × 40*

'E. Hoare' Foliage – deep green. Flower – bright red-purple in delicate sprays. Forms a low compact plant with the flower stems held above the foliage. Nice as a young plant but tends to get woody as it gets older. Mid-season. *20 × 38*

'Elegantissima, Walter Ingwersen' Foliage – mid-green. Flower – pink-lilac with individual florets larger than normal in extremely long delicate sprays. A selected plant brought back from Portugal by the late Mr Ingwersen and originally called 'Elegantissima'. Sited in the right place it is very beautiful but cannot be regarded as totally hardy. We have seen specimens similar to this growing shoulder high in Spain, although it would be nowhere near that in Britain. *50 × 30*

'Foxhollow Wanderer' Foliage – deep green. Flower – rose-lilac in long sprays. Vigorous, spreading in herring-bone fashion. A good plant for quick ground cover. *15 × 45*

[177]

'Foxii Floribunda' Foliage – emerald green. Flower – bright rose. Forms a tiny mound. *15 × 20*

'Foxii Nana' (83 and 107) Although similar to the foregoing, the true plant is tighter in growth and flowers are more infrequent which is no disadvantage, for the attraction is in the low hummock of bright green foliage. One of the smallest growers. *10 × 18*

'Goldsworth Crimson' Foliage – very dark green. Flower – red-purple in long spikes but generally rather thinly produced which is unfortunate as it is a good colour and flowers late. *38 × 45*

'Hibernica' Foliage – sparse, mid-green. Flower – lavender pink so profusely carried that the foliage is obscured. Twiggy, compact. Late. *25 × 25*

'Hiemalis' Foliage – dark green, rather hard to the touch. Flower – lilac pink in strong spikes. An excellent plant for a sheltered spot but not suitable for cold countries, for apart from the late flowering, the plant itself does not appear to be entirely hardy. *30 × 40*

'Hookstone' Foliage – bright green. Flower – clear pink. A young plant can produce extremely long spikes with the individual flowers spaced out over the whole length. Introduced by Underwoods, West End, Woking. *40 × 45*

'Hypnoides' Foliage – mid-green. Flower – short purple spikes. Compact. *20 × 25*

'Juno' (U.S.A.) Foliage – dense, mossy green, slightly hairy. Flower – short dense spikes of lavender flowers in profusion. Forms a mound of sturdy stems in an arching habit. Raised by Mayfair Nurseries who consider it to be a seedling of 'Sister Anne', and named after the owner's wife. *25 × 35*

'Kuphaldtii' Foliage – dark green. Flower – light purple. Plant grows in a completely prostrate manner with sparse twisting stems that form a twiggy mound. *8 × 25*

Another plant of German origin is 'Prostrata Flagelliformis' which is almost identical but larger in size.

'Loch-Na-Seil' Foliage – greyish-green. Flower – bright purple. Prostrate. *15 × 30*

'Lyndon Proudley' Foliage – fresh mid-green. Flower – lilac-pink in tight clusters on the short stems. A small-growing plant with minute foliage, suitable for the rock garden. We called this after our younger son. *20 × 25*

'Martha Hermann' (U.S.A.) Foliage – light green. Flower – white, shaded lilac in delicate upright sprays. Upright, moderately vigorous. *30 × 35*

'Minima' Foliage – bright green in summer turning dull green in winter. Flower – pale purple, but few. Low growing with dense spreading habit. Unfortunately, the growth, although prostrate, is rather floppy and the older plants are nearly always bare in the centre. *10 × 30*

'Minima, Smiths Variety' Foliage – pale green but can become rust-red during colder weather. Flower – pale lilac-pink in tiny spikes. Very slow growing. This worthwhile plant was found as a 'witches broom' on a normal plant in Ireland. *10 × 25*

'Mousehole' (109 and 117) Foliage – dark green, rather soft. Flower – very sparse light purple. Another miniature. This can be described as having a spiky appearance for the tiny foliage-clad stems radiate from the centre of the plant. Found by Mr and Mrs Letts while holidaying in Cornwall. *10 × 15*

†**'Mrs Ronald Gray'** Foliage – emerald green becoming dark green with age. Flower – pale purple appearing at the tips of the stems. Slow-growing prostrate carpeter. Found by the late Dr Ronald Gray of Hindhead and named after his first wife. *5 × 20*

'Mullion' (119) Foliage – dark green. Flower – rose-purple in abundance over a short period. Semi-prostrate, compact dome-shaped. Found by Mr and Mrs D. F. Maxwell near Mullion in Cornwall. Two other cultivars that are similar are 'Kynance' and 'Roma'. *25 × 35*

'Nana Compacta' Foliage – bright green. Flower – lilac-pink in tiny spikes. A miniature, slow to start but eventually forming a good-sized plant that always bears a good crop of flowers. *15 × 25*

'Pygmaea' Foliage – bright green. Flower – lilac-pink in tiny spikes. Very small growing and could almost be taken for 'Foxii Nana' when young but forms a more spreading plant with uneven growth. *8 × 20*

'Ralph Purnell' Foliage – dull green. Flower – reddish-purple on solid upright spikes. Tall, upright. Another of Mr Sparkes' introductions, and, when grown well, an imposing plant as well as an excellent cut flower. *30 × 30*

'Rosea' A very old cultivar name recently revived in the U.S.A. Foliage – light green. Flower – clear rose on curving spikes. A charming medium-sized grower. *25 × 40*

'Serlei Grandiflora' Foliage – dark green, soft plumose. Flower – reddish-purple. Very tall. Late. *40 × 50*

'Sister Anne' Foliage – soft thick greyish-green. Flower – pink in profusion. Of dense compact habit. *15 × 25*

'Spicata' (Holland) Foliage – pale green often with distinct purple tips. Flowers – light pink in tapering upright spikes. There are several similar forms in cultivation in Holland and Germany and the naming is rather confused. *30 × 35*

'Spicata Nana' A short growing plant. *25 × 35*

'Spicata Robusta' Strong, upright grower. *40 × 50*

'Tenuis' Foliage – dark green. Flower – deep scarlet flowering over a long period. Small and bushy. *20 × 25*

'Tom Thumb' Foliage – fresh mossy green. Flower – light pink. Small stiff upright habit with minute leaves and stems, seldom exceeds 20 cm in height. *15 × 20*

'Underwoodii' Foliage – mid-green. Flower – a haze of silvery-pink buds which never open. Delicate upright growth of medium height. Late. *30 × 45*

'Valorian' (U.S.A.) Foliage – dark green. Flower – short spikes of deep lavender flowers on horizontal stems. Prostrate and extremely dwarf, slowly forming a dense mat or slight mound, considered by the raisers to be intermediate between 'Mrs Ronald Gray' and 'Foxii Nana'. *20 × 30*

Coloured foliage and single-coloured flowers

'Andrew Proudley' (106) Foliage – yellow changing to tawny, with bronze and orange tints during winter. Flower – heavy clusters of purple-pink small flowers on tiny erect stems. A small shrubby little plant, considered a colour foliage counterpart of 'Lyndon Proudley' with the same tiny appearance making it an ideal choice for the rockery or trough garden.

We discovered this minute seedling in a pot of *Calluna* 'Lyndon Proudley' and can only surmise it was a seedling from it. Named after another of our children. *15 × 20*

'Aurea' (82) Foliage – light yellow-green. Young growth more golden with purplish tints becoming flushed rust red in colder weather. Flower – longish sprays of lilac-rose. An old cultivar still worth growing but not always long lived. *25 × 40*

'Blazeaway' Foliage – pale yellow-green with deep orange tints turning to brilliant red in winter on exposed surfaces of plant. Flower – pale mauve. Tall and upright. *30 × 35*

'Bonfire Brilliance' Foliage – brilliant yellow, orange and scarlet intensifying in winter. Flower – soft lilac. Fast growing and upright habit. *30 × 40*

'Boskoop' A seedling in Mr H. J. van de Laar's garden in Boskoop, Holland. Foliage – rich gold becoming orange-red in hard weather. Flowers lilac-rose in tapering spikes. This newcomer is midway in appearance between 'Blazeaway' and 'Robert Chapman'. We thought the foliage effect most impressive in the stock plants of Messrs. Zwijnenburg's Nursery in Boskoop. *30 × 35*

'Bunsall' Foliage – yellow in summer turning shades of bronze and pale orange in winter. Flower – palest lilac. Narrow upright branches. A seedling found by Mr George Osmond and named after the hamlet in which he lives. *30 × 35*

'Coral Island' Foliage – soft gold, orange tinted in summer, orange and red hues in winter. Flower – lavender. A vigorous yet dense growing seedling introduced by Mr Rawinsky of Haslemere. *25 × 30*

'Cuprea' Foliage – yellow and coppery tones, turning to bronzed red in winter. Flower – lilac. Slender and upright. Although an old cultivar is still one of the best and most popular. *30 × 40*

'Fairy' Foliage – yellow turning orange and gold in autumn and winter. Flower – pink. A new cultivar that appears to be quite compact in habit. *25 × 38*

'Golden Carpet' (20) Foliage – yellow with orange tints in winter. Flower – purple in short spikes. Prostrate, eventually forming a low hummock. *10 × 38*

'Golden Feather' (82) Foliage – soft yellow flushed orange on long feather-like plumes. Sometimes tinged deep orange and red in winter. Flower – seldom, mauve. Prostrate for the first season becoming more vigorous and spreading. 25 × 45

'Golden Rivulet' (43) Foliage – light yellow-gold turning orange in winter. Flower – lavender in arching spikes, sparse. Completely prostrate when young, this eventually develops into a plant rather like *C.v.* 'Golden Feather' in appearance but generally smaller. We have been told that in Holland it is preferred to the latter plant as it does not suffer the same amount of foliage scorch in the winter. Raised in Haslemere, Surrey, by Mr P. G. Davis. 20 × 30

'Hirsuta Typica' ('Incana') Foliage – glaucous green densely covered with silver hairs to give a silver-grey appearance. Flower – pale lilac rose, not prolific. Generally a little slow to establish, but then vigorous. Tall eventually. 30 × 45

'John F. Letts' Foliage – light yellow-gold, flecked orange and red. Colours intensifying in the colder weather. Flower – pale lavender, on tiny stems. Prostrate and low growing. One of two similar seedlings found in a bed of *C.v.* 'Mrs Ronald Gray' and named after the finder. This is the slower, smaller-growing plant, while 'Golden Carpet' has proved to be more vigorous. Makes a perfect plant for a bright splash on the winter rockery. 10 × 30

'Joy Vanstone' Foliage – pale gold with the merest hint of orange appearing towards autumn. Winter colour is bright gold with deep orange shades, sometimes banded with red. Flower – pale lilac mauve in long sprays. This distinct form raised by Mr Sparkes has a pleasing contrast between the silvery pink of the flowers against the soft yellow foliage. 28 × 35

†**'Multicolor'** Foliage – pale orange yellow turning deeper orange and red. Winter colour varies from red to dark purple with which the new growth in spring is displayed well. Flower – mauve in short spikes. Compact, low and bushy. Occasional green reversion should be removed when noticed. This colourful plant was raised in the States where it is known

as 'Prairie Fire' – an apt name. *15 × 30*

'Orange Queen' Foliage – pale yellow becoming soft orange with deeper-coloured tips. Flower – mauve in strong spikes. Upright habit of growth, especially good as a young plant, tending to lose its graceful appearance on maturity. *25 × 38*

'Oxshott Common' Foliage – glaucous green but covered in light hairs which provides the plant with a silvery sheen. Flower – lilac, but appears to be blue when viewed from a distance. Not as silver as 'Hirsuta Typica', but none the less very attractive when the long flowering spikes appear. Similar forms can be found almost anywhere on dry sandy commons, particularly near Chobham in Surrey. *35 × 45*

†**'Robert Chapman'** (78 and 130) Foliage – greenish yellow with orange-red tints. During autumn the orange intensifies and winter colour is brilliant red where exposed to frost and sun. Flower – bright mauve pink in moderate spikes. Upright compact shape with excellent foliage and is probably the most widely planted of this group. *25 × 40*

'Roland Haagen' (Holland) Foliage – bright yellow-gold changing to orange with bronze tips in the colder weather. Flowers – pale lavender. Mr Rinus Zwijnenburg, a Dutch nurseryman, found this originally as a sport on a wild green-leaved ling while on holiday in Ireland. Cuttings were taken back to Holland for rooting and the resulting plant named after a friend with him when the original find was made. *25 × 40*

'Rosalind' (113) Foliage – pale green becoming light golden-yellow in winter and often having terminal shoots of clear yellow or red. Flower – bright mauve in graceful sprays. Similar type of foliage and growth to the white-flowered 'Serlei'. Tall. Two varieties are grown, Crastock Heath and Underwood's, the latter generally regarded as the better foliage colour. *38 × 45*

'Silver Cloud' (42) Foliage – silvery-blue. Flower – light purple. Tight compact mound. We have a high regard for this lovely plant, probably the best to date for both its silver foliage, deep colour and floriferous habit. *15 × 30*

'Silver Knight' Foliage –

light silver-grey appearance. Flower – pale lilac rose in strong spikes. Upright and bushy. *35 × 40*

†'**Silver Queen**' (**81 and 104**) Foliage – green but completely overlaid with fine white hairs to give a grey or silver-blue effect. Flower – pinkish-lavender generally in long sprays. An exquisite plant that is of the greatest value for colour contrast. Much like 'Hirsuta Typica', possibly more upright and very vigorous under suitable conditions. *35 × 45*

†'**Sir John Charrington**' (**68**) Foliage – pale yellow-gold shaded orange with deeper orange tints during summer. Colour intensifies during autumn and winter to bright red on all exposed parts. Flower – deep maroon-purple in long graceful spikes.

This plant is the culmination of Mr Sparkes' efforts in producing outstanding coloured foliage forms of *Calluna*, for this has not only the beautiful foliage, but extremely good flowers as well. He presented it to Sir John Charrington on his eightieth birthday as a mark of respect and recognition of his work in the founding of the Heather Society, from having the original idea

and getting it launched. *25 × 40*

Rather similar is 'Gold Flame' which has slightly paler flowers and opens earlier.

'**Spitfire**' Foliage – delicate light greenish-yellow becoming pale golden with reddish tints. Winter colour intense red where exposed to sun and frost. Flower – light mauve in dainty long sprays. *25 × 40*

'**Summer Orange**' Foliage – light yellow, more orange towards tips. Colour intensifies considerably in winter months. Flower – soft lilac rose in dainty sprays. Slender upright habit. One of the most valuable for both summer and winter colour. *30 × 40*

'**Sunset**' (**101, 118 and 126**) Foliage – pale yellow with orange and red tints becoming bright red in winter. Flower – pale pink, rather few on short sprays. Rather like 'Robert Chapman' but more open growth which tends to arch downwards. *30 × 40*

'**Wickwar Flame**' Foliage – gold and orange, deep orange and flame in winter. Flower – pale rose in short spikes. Very vigorous as a young plant, about midway in appearance between 'Golden Feather' and 'Robert Chapman', with outstanding winter colour. Raised by Mr G. Osmond of Wickwar, Gloucestershire. *30* × *40*

'Winter Chocolate' Foliage – greenish-yellow and orange becoming golden yellow with orange tips, finally dark chocolate with red tips. Flower – lilac pink, few. Growth is close, compact but ultimately bushy. *25* × *30*

Coloured flowers – double
'Baby Wicklow' A sport from 'County Wicklow' found by Mr Dick Boer of Boskoop, Holland, this must hold the record among heathers for being the smallest grower ever! Forming a tight dark green mound of closely packed shoots it has a few flowers similar in appearance to the parent but on a much reduced scale. *5* × *10*

'Carl Röders' An interesting early flowering sport found on the Luneberg Heath, Northern Germany, in 1960 and introduced by Mr H. Westermann. The flowers are pink with a hint of mauve and carried profusely. *20* × *30*

'County Wicklow' (**70**) ('Camla') Foliage – light green, darker in winter. Flower – soft pink in rather short, closely packed spikes. These can remain attractive for three months or more. Semi-prostrate and compact. One of the finest heathers and suitable for even the smallest garden. *20* × *30*

'Elsie Purnell' (**129**) Foliage – silver green. Flower – soft rose with white centres in solid, very long spikes – especially so in a young plant. Mr Sparkes raised this plant from a sport on 'H. E. Beale' more for his own use in his cut-flower business than for garden purposes. Many regard it as an improvement on the original for the generally longer stems. Flowering about two weeks later than 'H. E. Beale' a well-grown plant presents a magnificent sight. *40* × *45*

'Flore Pleno' (**86 and 102**) Foliage – dull, dark green, often purplish in winter. Flower – lilac-rose in distinctly tapering spikes. A compact grower and although the first double ling to be included in nurserymen's lists is still worthy of a place in the garden today. Needs to have the old flower spikes removed to keep it in good shape. *30* × *35*

'H. E. Beale' (**99, 120, 126 and 128**) Foliage – grey-green, rather sparse. Flower – long sprays of pale silvery pink, deepening to rose with paler centres. Vigorous, and provided it is kept growing by good cultivation will produce a wonderful display for many years. Raised from a wild 'find' in the New Forest and sent to Maxwell and Beale's Nursery for propagating. Hundreds of thousands must have been raised and sold from these two original cuttings which arrived at the nursery in a shrivelled state. *38 × 45*

'**Ingrid Bouter**' Foliage – dark green. Flower – fully double, deep clear red in delicate sprays, upright. An extremely long flowering plant that originated as a sport on cultivar 'Tib'. *25 × 35*

†'**J. H. Hamilton**' Foliage – dark green. Flower – clear bright pink in dainty sprays. The cut stems last well when dried and used for winter decoration in vases. Compact grower, more spreading than upright, succeeding well in heavy soils as do many of the other double heathers. *15 × 30*

'**Jimmy Dyce**' Foliage – dark green, tinged reddish in cold weather. Flower – bright pinkish purple, individual florets rounded, in short, very slender spikes. A short growing, rather tufted plant

that is in flower for many weeks. Found by Mr Dyce who was leading a party of members of the British Pteridological Society (a society devoted to the study of ferns and their allies) who were botanizing in Norfolk. *15 × 25*

'**Joan Sparkes**' Foliage – bright green. Flower – lilac-pink on dainty stems. Growth is compact but becomes wide-spreading in suitable soils. Flowering branches tend to hang down with the weight of the flowers on a young plant which can become damaged in wet weather. This slight problem disappears as the plant matures and growth is more bushy and upright. *23 × 35*

†'**Peter Sparkes**' (**75 and 76**) Foliage – dark grey-green. Flower – deep pink in strong spikes. A beautiful form in which the fully double florets are also carried on short laterals at the base of the main spike. Deeper in colour than 'H. E. Beale' from which it was said to be a sport. ['Cramond' – shorter growing and widespread, possibly even deeper in colour, and 'Glencoe' are recently introduced cultivars similar in general appearance.] *38 × 45*

'**Radnor**' ('Miss Appleby')

Foliage – dark green. Flower – silvery-lilac in short densely packed spikes. Compact, floriferous resembling the older 'Flore Pleno' in form but having a lighter colour. Anyone that finds 'County Wicklow' difficult or slow should try this as it seems to be an easy grower. Discovered locally by Miss H. M. Appleby of Presteigne, Radnor, it was sent to Dingle Hollow Nursery, Cheshire for trial, more for the reddish coloration of the foliage (which seems not to have been maintained) than for the delightful double flowers. There it was known simply as 'Radnor Variety' (from Miss Appleby) and various nurserymen acquiring stock call the plant 'Radnor' and others 'Miss Appleby'. *20 × 30*

Single-coloured flowers – coloured new growth

'Fred J. Chapple' Foliage – dark green with new growth of bright yellow with pink or red tips, eventually becoming cream flushed pink. Flower – lilac mauve in strong spikes. *30 × 38*

Other similar cultivars are 'Tricolorifolia' and 'Hammondii Rubrifolia', the latter being dwarfer.

'Mrs Alf' Foliage – dark brick-red against deep green in spring. Flower – pale pink Bushy, forms a twiggy, compact plant. Coloured foliage display is rather brief – three weeks at most. *15 × 30*

'Mrs Pat' (33) Foliage – new growth is pink which turns white and finally light green flecked with white. Tips bright red in winter. Flower – graceful sprays of silvery pink. Kept growing well this dainty plant can produce a good display at any time of the year but is generally at its best during the spring. Neat, dwarf habit. *15 × 30*

'Sally-Anne Proudley' Foliage – clear yellow tipped sealing-wax red, becoming cream and then dark green speckled with white. Mature foliage is very dark green. Flower – pale lavender, late. A compact, upright grower. The spring display was once aptly described as being like a 'miniature Christmas tree covered in fairy lights'. Named after our only daughter. *25 × 25*

'Spring Torch' Foliage – in spring is yellow-shaded apricot, darker towards the ends. Adult foliage is greyish-green. Flower – pale lilac rose in long spikes. The colourful display is outstanding for a few weeks but then becomes rather uninteresting. *25 × 30*

'Spring Glow' is almost identical to the foregoing.

ERICA MULTIFLORA
(Many-flowered heath)
A shrubby plant that occurs around much of the south and central Mediterranean coast and the Atlantic coast of Morocco. When we first saw this growing in the rocky hillsides near the sea in southern France we thought how similar it was to the Cornish heath – *E. vagans*. On closer inspection we found that the racemes of pinkish flowers are looser with each bell being held on a long pedicel. On older plants the flowers appear more as terminal clusters, and are in varying shades. This can be from almost white to mauve-pink in the wild although the cultivated is generally clear pink. This does not have a cultivar name at present although it should. Certainly not as hardy as *E. vagans* and cannot be recommended for outside cultivation over all of Britain nor in those countries where winter protection is needed for the 'hardy heaths'. Height – ultimately to a metre. After three years *30 × 30*. Flowering time is autumn and winter.

INDEX

Numbers in bold type refer to the colour plates